The problem of "Hamlet"

J M. 1856-1933 Robertson

Dipak Nandy

NOTTINGHAM
1998

THE PROBLEM
OF
"HAMLET"

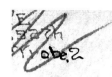

THE PROBLEM
OF
"HAMLET"

BY

J. M. ROBERTSON

Author of "Shakespeare and Chapman,"
"The Baconian Heresy," etc.

LONDON: GEORGE ALLEN & UNWIN LTD
RUSKIN HOUSE, 40 MUSEUM STREET, W.C. 1

First published in 1919

PREFACE

FOR some years, as a result of a lifetime rather largely devoted to Shakespeare study, the author has been engaged on a work on " The Canon of Shakespeare," designed to deal with all the problems coming under that title. In 1905 he preluded the undertaking with a volume entitled " Did Shakespeare write TITUS ANDRONICUS ? " which, rewritten and greatly expanded, he hopes shortly to reissue as a practical introduction to the study of the entire " Canon." The whole ground, it is hoped, need not be covered on the same scale ; and a number of the more problematic plays have been dealt with in sections of moderate length. The complete work, however—if the author should live to complete it—will inevitably be a bulky one ; and he hopes, before putting it in a final form, to have the benefit of expert criticism of at least a number of the sections.

It is proposed, accordingly, to issue some of them separately. This course has already been begun by the publication of the volume SHAKESPEARE AND CHAPMAN (1917), which sets forth the most revolutionary of the critical inferences to which the author has thus far been led, and which involves a fresh consideration of the origins of a number of the Plays. One of those there referred to has since been fully discussed in the paper on "The Problem of THE MERRY WIVES OF WINDSOR," published for the Shakespeare Association (Chatto & Windus). The present volume, which reviews and attempts to resolve the most interesting and the most extensive debate relating to any of them, is submitted as an illustration of what is claimed to be the proper method of investigating all, for the given purpose.

Only since my MS. was put in the hands of the printer have I received Mr. J. Dover Wilson's interesting and valuable contributions to the inquiry entitled "The Copy for 'Hamlet,' 1603, and the 'Hamlet' Transcript, 1593" (A. Moring, Ltd., 1918). Coinciding, I think, in the main with my view, that investigation opens up several correlative questions; and I have thought it well to await the further inquiry promised by Mr. Wilson before attempting to connect his results with mine.

March 1919.

CONTENTS

THE PROBLEM OF "HAMLET"

I

THE ÆSTHETIC PROBLEM

§ 1. Subjective Theories.

THERE is no better illustration of the need for a study of the genesis of the Shakespeare Plays than the endless discussion of the æsthetic problem of HAMLET. It has continued for two centuries, latterly with the constant preoccupation of finding a formula which shall reduce the play to æsthetic consistency; and every solution in turn does but ignore some of the data which motived the others. All alike are inconclusive, because all ignore in effect, even when they make mention of it, the essential fact that Shakespeare's HAMLET is an adaptation of an older play, which laid down the main action, embodying a counter-sense which the adaptation could not transmute. To constate the successive theses is to make this clear.

The formula put by Goethe in WILHELM MEISTER'S LEHRJAHRE—that the tragedy is one of an overwhelming task laid upon a spirit incapable of it [1]—is, to begin

---

[1] " To me it is clear that Shakespeare meant to present a great deed laid upon a soul that is not capable of it. . . . Here is an oak-tree planted in a costly vase that should have nurtured only lovely flowers : the roots expand ; the vase is shattered."—*Lehrjahre*, B. iv, Cap. xiii, end. Cp. Cap. iii.

11

with, an imperfect substitute for that put by Henry Mackenzie in his essay in the Edinburgh MIRROR (No. 99) in 1780.[1] Already in Mackenzie's day it was common ground that " Of all the characters of Shakespeare, that of Hamlet has been generally thought the most difficult to be reduced to any fixed or settled principle " ; and Mackenzie set himself " to inquire whether any leading idea can be found, upon which these apparent contradictions may be reconciled." He found it in " an extreme sensibility of mind, apt to be strongly impressed by its situation, and overpowered by the feelings which that situation excites." The terrible circumstances unhinged those " principles of action which in a happier situation would have yielded a happy life." Hamlet's character is thus " often variable and uncertain," and the suggestion is offered that " this is the very character which Shakespeare meant to allot to him." " Finding such a character in real life, of a person endowed with feelings so delicate as to border on weakness, with sensibility too exquisite to allow of determined action," he " has placed it where it could be best exhibited, in scenes of wonder, of terror, of imagination."

This " subjective " theorem, which best of all provides for the various contingencies, anticipates and transcends both that of Goethe,[2] which might be the formula of a hundred tragedies, and that of Schlegel and Coleridge—

[1] Professor Herford, in his paper on " Recent Contributions to Shakespeare Criticism " in the *Book of Homage* (p. 182), while noting that Goethe's criticism is misleading and in some of its implications quite wrong, pronounces that it " virtually started the Hamlet problem." This, as we shall see, holds only for Goethe's own age. The discussion goes back to Gildon at least.

[2] As Hermann Türck remarks (*Das psychologische Problem in der Hamlet-Tragödie*, 1894, p. 8), Goethe's view of Hamlet is an account of his own Werther, whom Türck describes almost in Mackenzie's formula as a nature " yielding to every impression."

that Hamlet is the victim of an excess of the reflective faculty, which unfits him for action. The answer to both of these was given in 1828 by Coleridge's son Hartley,[1] who pointed out that " feebleness of mind, the fragility of a china vase, lack of power and energy, are not the characteristics of Hamlet. So far from it, he is represented as fearless, almost above the strength of humanity. He does not ' set his life at a pin's fee '." Hartley in turn proffered the formula that " it is not the weight and magnitude, the danger and difficulty of the deed imposed as a duty, that weighs upon his soul and enervates the sinews of his moral being, but the preternatural contradiction involved in the duty itself, the irregular means through which the duty is promulgated and known." In short, Shakespeare's purpose was " to show the evil and confusion which must be introduced into the moral world by a sensible communication between natural and supernatural beings."[2]

This thesis, which is confuted by the TEMPEST and the DREAM, has never made any avowed converts ; but the denial of Hamlet's alleged weakness of nature has often been repeated, and must many times have been made by independent English students before and after Hartley Coleridge, as it was by Ulrici (as he supposed, for the first time) in 1839, and after him by many other Germans,[3] down to our own day. Nevertheless, the

---

[1] In the essay *On the Character of Hamlet*, in *Blackwood's Magazine*, reprinted in *Essays and Marginalia*, 1851, i. 151 sq. ·
[2] Essay on *Shakespeare a Tory and a Gentleman*, vol. cited, p. 144.
[3] See his *Shakespeare's Dramatic Art*, Eng. trans. 1876, i. 483, *note*. Goethe's thesis is now almost universally given up. Gervinus, however, in 1850 could still write : " Since this riddle has been solved by Goethe in his Wilhelm Meister, it is scarcely to be conceived that it ever was one."—*Shakespeare Commentaries*, Eng. trans, i. 109.

kindred doctrine that Hamlet delayed his action because
he could not make up his mind has continued to appear
in critical literature, and still has many adherents.
Lowell, taking it over from Coleridge, held it as a fixed
dogma, and imposed it in his eloquent essay SHAKESPEARE
ONCE MORE, in some respects the most influential study
of Shakespeare in its generation. Lowell alludes to the
old story from which the play derives, and he must have
known that the critics inferred a pre-Shakespearean
play; but he confidently proceeds on the assumption
that Shakespeare's conception of Hamlet's character
" was the ovum out of which the whole organism was
hatched," finding even that " Hamlet seems the natural
result of the mixture of the father and mother in this
temperament, the resolution and persistence of the one,
like sound timber worm-holed and made shaky, as it
·were, by the other's infirmity of will and discontinuity
of purpose."

Thus is assigned to the victim of heredity both resolution and irresolution; while the " temperament,"
with an " imagination in overplus " that has no heredity,
determines the action all the same. Hamlet, accordingly, is duly scolded through many pages, with no
attempt to face either conflicting data or conflicting
theories. So strange an anomaly as the occurrence of
the " To be " soliloquy after the ghost scene is merely
turned to the account of the indictment: " He doubts
the immortality of the soul after seeing his father's
spirit "—a flat misrepresentation. What Hamlet does
is to say that " no traveller returns "—which constitutes
an anomaly in the construction of the play, not in Hamlet's
" character."

All the while, Lowell does not believe that Shakespeare

wrote this or any of his plays with a " didactic purpose."
The implication would seem to be that the dramatist
left that to his readers, simply providing a hero who
could be scolded, as never was hero before, by literary
persons conscious of their own consummate fitness for
killing a guilty uncle at a moment's notice. " If we
must draw a moral from Hamlet," writes Lowell, " it
would seem to be that Will is Fate, and that, Will once
abdicating, the inevitable successor is the regency of
Chance. Had Hamlet acted instead of musing how good
it would be to act, the king might have been the only
victim. As it is, all the main actors in the story are
the fortuitous sacrifice of his irresolution." With a
fine unconsciousness, the critic has previously observed :
" With what perfect tact and judgment Shakespeare,
in the advice to the players, makes him an exquisite
critic ! " And yet subsequent exquisite critics, as we
see, are quite confident that they have escaped the
" great vice of character " they assign to Shakespeare's
prince. No one thinks it necessary to vituperate Macbeth
for slaying Duncan, or Othello for murdering Desdemona ;
still less is Desdemona denounced for prevaricating about
her handkerchief and thereby entailing her own and
Othello's death ; but for *not* killing Claudius either at
the start or in the praying scene, Hamlet has been the
theme of a hundred denunciations by zealous moralists.
It would be odd if Shakespeare, who, says Lowell, " never
acted without unerring judgment," had deliberately
planned for that.

At this point we may fitly pause to note the singular
unanimity, preserved down to our own day, with which
the critics of all schools have taken for granted that Hamlet
does in a remarkable way delay his revenge. To judge

from their language, he procrastinates to a degree that calls for an explanation; and the burden of their testimony is either that no explanation is given or that it lies in his character, temperament, or mood. And all the while, unless we decide that Hamlet's duty, after hearing the Ghost's tale, is to proceed *instantly* to slay the king, there has been as little delay as might well be! It is solely as regards the interval between Acts I and II that a charge can be laid. There has been time for the journey of the ambassadors from Denmark to Norway and back, and for Polonius to think of sending Reynaldo to inquire about Laertes' doings in Paris. But it is not upon this interval, or upon Hamlet's quiescence therein, that the stress of criticism has fallen, though it is only in this period, of which we see nothing, that Hamlet can be said to have shown any sensitive recoil from the act of vengeance. The latest critic to revive that charge, Professor W. F. Trench, after sternly censuring Hamlet for being " unable to decide upon a course of action " and for " resolving to let himself go " after the Ghost scene,[1] expressly pronounces[2] that " at the end of Act II, Fate is still well disposed to Hamlet." That is to say, there has been no deadly delay up to the point at which Hamlet, retrospectively hesitating to believe in the Ghost, plans the court play.

On that view, the " procrastination " of Hamlet resolves itself into the single abstention from slaying the king while he prays. Having made up his mind that the hero's sole faculty is to talk and " preach," the critic scornfully comments that when Hamlet resheathes his

[1] *Shakespeare's Hamlet: A New Commentary*, 1913, p. 87.
[2] *Id.* p. 127.

sword he has " caught sight of and grasped an excuse for procrastinating *once more* ; " [1] which must mean either that Hamlet ought to have killed the king *at* the play a few minutes before, or that his previous delay had after all been unpardonable. At once we are moved to put the two questions whether king-killing is supposed to be usually accomplished with the extreme promptitude here insisted on ; and whether any stage-character but Hamlet has ever been subjected to such a rigour of criticism. And if, further, we do but ask ourselves what kind of a moral and what kind of an æsthetic effect would have been secured by Hamlet's stabbing the king in the back while he knelt at prayer, we may be led to question yet further whether the moral efficiency of Hamlet is not after all rather higher than that of his censors.

Save for that one episode, wherein, whatever be supposed to be the real motive, procrastination is simple decency, the choice to kill manfully at another time rather than to stab in the back, there is no further " delay " on Hamlet's part, the action proceeding breathlessly up to his deportation, to be resumed on his return, whereafter he can be accused of procrastination only by those who argue that he ought at the very outset to have proved his manhood by raising the mob as did Laertes, the type of headlong precipitation. Considered from the standpoint of practical politics, even of assassination politics, Hamlet's " delay " is negligible ; while his faculty for volition and action would seem to be sufficiently proved by his murderously prompt disposal of Polonius and the two courtiers, and his boarding of the pirate ship.

[1] *Id.* p. 171.

2

But one thing must be said for the critics. Shakespeare himself has in a manner given them their warrant, by the two vivid soliloquies in which he makes Hamlet impeach himself. And this the dramatist has done partly on a cue from the old play, partly in virtue of his own idiosyncrasy of idealistic disregard of time. Under circumstances which we shall discuss later, he took up the old play which he has transmuted, and finding in it an action that to his time-discounting sense was one of unexplained delay (being so felt by Hamlet himself on the second visitation of the Ghost in the old play), elaborated that aspect of the hero as he did every other. In all likelihood he was responding to an impression of the theatre which chimed with his idiosyncrasy—revealed in the impossible treatment of time in OTHELLO and MEASURE FOR MEASURE, to name no others.[1] That Hamlet " shilly-shallied " was in all likelihood the verdict of the audiences before the critics made it their theme ; because the " two hours' traffic of the stage " psychologically predisposes us to an exigence which in reading a novel we should not think of practising. So much must happen in so short a space that normal standards of criticism of conduct are cast aside ; and inasmuch as Shakespeare in his adaptation assented to this, treating Hamlet as one who inexplicably procrastinated, the litigation set up by the critics must be allowed to proceed. But, in the interest alike of Shakespeare and of critical science, it must be logically conducted to the end ; and this, as we have seen and shall see further, has not been

---

[1] Whether this telescoping of time is specially a result of the dramatist's adaptation of other men's work is a problem which calls for separate treatment. It has also to be asked whether the academic insistence on the " unities " moved him to evade the proper indications of time-interval.

done. What has been achieved is but a series of conflicting propositions, all professing to sum up the case without facing all the facts.

§ 2. Objective Theories.

After the rebuttal of the Goethean formula of temperamental incompetence,[1] the next step was to frame a formula of *objective* hindrances which delayed Hamlet's revenge. In 1845, George Fletcher, in an article in the WESTMINSTER REVIEW,[2] dwelt on the overpowering force of the obstacles; and made an allusion to the "preternatural embarrassment of the most horrible kind superadded," which points back to Hartley Coleridge. In 1846 J. L. Klein, the German historian of modern drama, set forth in the BERLINER MODENSPIEGEL the thesis that Hamlet was barred from action by the manner of the crime and the nature of his knowledge of it, which could not be offered as evidence to justify an assassination of the guilty king. Another German, Levinstein, is cited as putting the same view before Werder. Professor Karl Werder, in turn, independently framed and expounded the same thesis in his lectures on HAMLET at the Berlin University in 1859-60, and again in 1871-2.[3]

[1] Lowell, having plumped for the formula of Schlegel and Coleridge, naturally joined in deprecating that of Goethe, observing that he " seems to have considered the character too much from one side," but does not argue the point at all well. Hamlet, he remarks, " was hardly a sentimentalist " like Werther. On Goethe's side it might be replied that Lowell makes him very truly a sentimentalist, in that he lives in sentiment and is finally determined to action by " chance."

[2] Reprinted in *Studies of Shakespeare* in 1847. Furness does not note this essay in his Variorum edition ; and Rolfe, who cites it in his 1903 ed. of *Hamlet* and in his introduction to Miss Wilder's translation of Werder (Putnams, 1907), does not mention Hartley Coleridge.

[3] Lectures published in full in the *Preussische Jahrbücher*, 1873-4, and reprinted in book form, 1875 and 1893.

Even as the champions of the subjective theory, impressed by the evidence of Hamlet's procrastination, ignored that of his faculty for prompt and vigorous action, so the champions of the objective theory, impressed by that evidence, dwelt on the insurmountable difficulties of Hamlet's task, and ignored his own self-accusations. Werder, whose prolix and declamatory handling of a fairly plausible thesis reveals its inadequacy to a considerate reader, seems to have made many converts, including Furness, Hudson, Corson and Rolfe,[1] all of whom, like him, took for granted the thoroughly planned character of the play, though they admitted minor perplexities. But it is precisely on the view of a thorough plan that their thesis most completely breaks down. If in Shakespeare's view Hamlet was faced by insuperable difficulties of circumstance, it was Shakespeare's plain business to let us see as much. And this he never once does. His Hamlet " does not know," any more than we, why his task recedes from him.

Surprisingly popular latterly in the United States, Werder's theory had small success among European critics, in Germany or elsewhere. It is marked by the " vigour and rigour " which Arnold ascribed to German theories in general, the tactic of driving the thesis anyhow through or over the facts which is so characteristic of German publicism—and politics. Of his own thesis Werder writes : " That this point for a century long should never have been seen is the most incomprehensible thing that has ever happened in æsthetic criticism from the very beginning of its existence "—a kind of vocifer-

[1] Mr. W. H. Widgery (*Harness Prize Essays on the First Quarto of* '*Hamlet*,' 1880, p. 185 sq.) adopted the position.

ation that does not usually accompany real discoveries. The stress of Werder's case lies on the position that a mere killing of the king would not only put Hamlet himself in danger from the indignant people but would wholly fail to secure his real end—the *judicial* conviction and execution of the murderer. To the retort that Hamlet never once indicates any such ideal, Werder replies that the "state of the case" speaks for him; and to the further retort that such an argument is merely a *petitio principii* his genial supporter, Mr. W. J. Rolfe, replies that the "subjective" theorists, who oppose, argue in the same fashion.[1] That is doubtless true; but Werder's thesis is not thereby to be established.

Professor Tolman, who regretfully rejects Werder's solution, leaves it intact by merely countering with the subjective theory—"Character" as against "Fate." The complete or general answer to Werder is that not only is his explanation nowhere indicated in the play, not only is his conception of the need for a judicial punishment alien to the whole ethic and atmosphere of the play, but it comes to the same thing as the subjective theory in that it makes Hamlet recoil from the possible course and fasten on an impossible one. How should the king be convicted? On his own evidence, under torture? A public investigation is the last thing Hamlet could critically be supposed to wish; and neither his pictured compatriots nor the Elizabethan audience can be conceived as craving for it. Above all, the audience. Yet Werder is as insistent for his arbitrary hypothesis as he is blind to the case for the subjective

[1] Introd. to *The Heart of Hamlet's Mystery* (trans. of Werder's lectures, 1907), p. 18.

theory. In the closet scene, he observes [1] "the Ghost
says *only* :

> Do not forget. This visitation
> Is but to whet *thy almost blunted purpose.*"

Only! We are apparently invited to suppose that the
Ghost, like all the subjective critics, was mistaken! Rolfe,
most lovable of Shakespeareans, actually meets Professor
Bradley's challenge to face the text by saying that
an external obstacle is " clearly implied " in Hamlet's

> Sith I have cause and will and strength and *means*
> To do't——

the very lines that are preceded by

> *I do not know*
> Why yet I live to say, 'This thing's to do.'

And against the challenge to explain away Hamlet's
phrases about his " sword " and his " arm," Rolfe affirms
that the words are used " *because* the *killing* of the king
is the end or aim of his task," which must wait " until
he can ' bring the king to *public justice.*' " It suffices
to confront this, once more, with Hamlet's words in the
praying scene :—

> Up, sword, and know thou a more horrid hent :
> *When he is drunk, asleep, or in his rage,*
> *Or in the incestuous pleasures of his bed ;*
> *At gaming, swearing, or about some act*
> *That has no relish of salvation in't :*
> *Then trip him,* that his heels may kick at heaven . . .

---

[1] Trans. cited, p. 47.

Before this, the " public justice " theory simply disappears, even as does the subjective theory before the challenge of Hamlet's slaughterous acts, though that theory naturally fastens on the lines before us as indicating a recoil from the decisive action needed.

Well may Rolfe avow that " All the theories, whether subjective or objective, have their difficulties." [1] Those of the theory he embraces, however, are the most obvious and most instantly fatal of all. Framed and adopted because of the failure of the subjective theory in any of its forms to meet the data, it reveals itself as still worse founded than they; and it accordingly makes by far the worse figure in debate. Admitted by its adherents to fail in meeting all the difficulties, and raising as it does new difficulties of the most hopeless kind, it compels us to seek sounder ground.

§ 3. Theory of Defect in the Dramatist.

Both the subjective and the objective explanations being so obviously inadequate to the data, the capable Gustav Rümelin (afterwards Kanzler of Tübingen) in his SHAKESPEARESTUDIEN, published in book form in 1866, countered the critics in general with a thesis of " faults of the poet " as against alike that of " faults of the hero " and the claim to justify the play as a whole. Bent on countering " Shakespeare-Mania " in the centenary year 1864, Rümelin was more concerned to impugn Shakespeare's work than to explain it ; and he in turn,

[1] Rolfe is quaintly at strife with his leader on one point. On the " times are out of joint " speech he writes (p. 37) : " Most significant words, though the critics have taken little note of them." In the same volume (p. 108) we find Werder writing : " Critics have made too much of these words."

though he pointed to the old Hamlet-saga as conditioning Shakespeare's play, did not substantiate his case by the data as to the pre-Shakespearean tragedy of Kyd. On the other hand, Hebler, who resisted alike Rümelin and Werder, continued to maintain a position [1] in which the dilemmas of the play were partly ignored.

Rümelin's position, as it happened, had long been anticipated by British common-sense. Gildon in 1710 had charged on the play " abundance of errors in ,the conduct and design," insisting, that " Shakespeare was master of this story," and therefore responsible for the plot. Hanmer in 1730, in turn, pronounced that " our poet by keeping too close to the groundwork of his plot has fallen into an absurdity "; adding " Had Hamlet gone naturally to work . . . there would have been an end of our play. The poet, therefore, was obliged to delay his hero's revenge ; but then he *should have contrived some good reason for it.*" [2] And Mackenzie in 1780 confessed of the dramatist : " Of the structure of his stories, or the probability of his incidents, he is frequently careless "; and again : " It may perhaps be doing Shakespeare no injustice to suppose that he sometimes began a play without having fixed in his mind, in any determined manner, the plan or conduct of his piece."

The same caveat was otherwise put by Edgar Poe :

In all commentating upon Shakespeare there has been a radical error never yet mentioned. It is the error of attempting to expound

---

[1] *Aufsätze über Shakespeare*, 2te Aufl. 1872.

[2] Cited by Malone, Var. ed. at end of play. Professor Bradley has, I think, done Hanmer injustice (*Shakespearean Tragedy*, 2nd ed. p. 91) by not citing the last sentence. It is in perfect accord with his own avowal (p. 93) that the psychological unintelligibility of a dramatic character " shows only the incapacity or folly of the dramatist." We shall see that these expressions are in the present case unduly severe.

his characters, to account for their actions, to reconcile their inconsistencies, not as if they were the coinage of a human brain, but as if they had been actual existences upon earth. We talk of Hamlet the man, instead of Hamlet the *dramatis persona*—of Hamlet that God, in place of Hamlet that Shakespeare created. . . . It is not . . . the inconsistencies of the acting man which we have as a subject of discussion . . . but the whims and vacillations, the conflicting energies and indolences of the poet. It seems to us little less than a miracle that this obvious point should have been overlooked.[1]

Needless to say, it had not been universally overlooked, having been clearly put more than a century before Poe by Gildon and Hanmer, and again by Mackenzie ; but when Hartley Coleridge said : " Let us, for a moment, put Shakespeare out of the question, and consider Hamlet as a real person, a recently deceased acquaintance," he was asking us to do what most of the later critics have commonly done, to the miscarriage of the problem. It is the course taken by Professor W. F. Trench in his commentary on the play, which only incidentally suggests possibilities of confusion in Shakespeare's work, and never at all contemplates the problem of adaptation of a previous play. This partly holds good, in fact, even of the admirable study of Professor Bradley, who so conclusively confutes alike the old subjective theory and the modern objective theory of Hamlet's procrastination, and so judicially, to my thinking, substitutes in effect, although he does not consistently adhere to, the explanation of psychic shock (if I may so phrase it) as being alone broadly compatible with the data. Hamlet, in short, as we see him, is neither weak of spirit nor really outmatched by mere circumstance. Even Werder falls back chronically on subjective solutions, as, for instance, that Hamlet feels at certain stages that he is not getting

[1] *Marginalia : Addenda :* Works, ed. Ingram, iv. 469–70.

help " from above "—a thesis as entirely gratuitous as
the formula that Rosencrantz and Guildenstern perish
partly because " they are not serving God "[1] This is
the theorist's way of discounting the fact that Hamlet
avows his own unjustified abstention from action.
Granting the theatrical view that there *has* been a surprising abstention, the candid course, though not the
final solution, is to say with Professor Bradley that something *in* or undergone by Hamlet withholds him from
the act of revenge ; and that this something is clearly
not mere over-reflection, even though Hamlet does talk of

> Some craven scruple
> Of thinking too precisely on the event,
> A thought which, quarter'd, hath but one part wisdom,
> And ever three parts coward.

The point is that after all his self-analysis he avows :.

> *I do not know*
> Why yet I live to say ' This thing's to do ';
> Sith I have cause and *will* and *strength* and *means*
> To do't.

And the conclusion must apparently be, *if* we are to
frame a theory of " the man Hamlet " at all, that for
his soul, poisoned by the knowledge of his mother's guilt,
the act of vengeance is really no solace, fiercely as he
craves it from time to time. Life for him remains
poisoned, there being nothing that can fully revive his
will-to-live after that deadly injury. An adequate love-
motive is lacking, Ophelia being inadequacy incarnate.
For Hamlet, life is not worth living, and revenge is not

---

[1] *The Heart of Hamlet's Mystery*, trans. cited, p. 169.

worth taking save by way of final closing of the whole account.

But this comparatively just though incomplete induction, to which the Germanic ethic of Werder made him blind, is probably obscured for those who follow him by reason simply of their habit of seeing HAMLET as a planned play, not as a play of adaptation and adjustment. We now know that such it was. Goethe's account of the piece as something suddenly and wonderfully conceived by the poet [1] we now know to be a pure chimera; and Goethe would have confessed as much if he had been told the play's history. And Professor Bradley, who, if I read him aright, is at times in accord with the construction above put, stops short, for the same reason, of the verdict that HAMLET is not finally an intelligible drama as it stands, though he nearly pronounces it. That verdict we must face. Hanmer is finally quite right : the poet *as dramatist*, having actually put in Hamlet's mouth a repeated avowal of inexplicable delay, should have given us a reason for it. And he does not, precisely because his transmutation of the play was but a process of making more and more mysterious a delay which in the earlier story was not mysterious at all. In the early story there *were* " objective " reasons for Hamlet's delay, and these have been progressively eliminated, leaving the harmonists to invent new. In the early story Hamlet makes no self-accusals : these have been expressly inserted, so that the harmonists are moved to invent explanations. But explanations are just what the dramatist has neither inserted nor indicated.

Those who argue that a reason is in any way *given* are invariably found either to ignore or do violence to

[1] Eckermann, *Gespräche*, 1828, 11 März.

features of the play which conflict with their interpretation, or to impose upon it and us a thesis which the
whole play rejects. The latest experimenters conform
to the rule. Thus the Rev. Dr. H. Ford, in his SHAKE-
SPEARE'S HAMLET : A NEW THEORY (1900), claiming to
show " what was the poet's intention in the play," argues
that Hamlet's inhibition, lies in his knowledge that
Christianity vetoed revenge.[1] Yet of such a conception
or motive there is not one hint in the entire play. On
the contrary, not only does Hamlet many times vow
revenge and never once avow hesitation about its fitness :
he *takes* revenge on Rosencrantz and Guildenstern without a sign of subsequent remorse, whereupon Dr. Ford
declares that the deed " needs no apology. A justifiable
act of self-defence " [which it emphatically was not]
" carries with it no self-reproach." [2] And besides thus
substantially upsetting his own thesis, the theorist incidentally suggests that, " though conscience repels the
thought of revenge, Hamlet nevertheless uses conscience
as *a kind of subterfuge and excuse for not doing what he
has no intention of doing.*" [3] *Solvuntur tabulæ.* For the
rest, the critic also argues, as so many had done before
him, that Hamlet before his knowledge of the murder
is already shattered by his mother's incestuous marriage [4]
—all this by way of repelling the formula of " irresolution," which he mistakenly supposed to be so generally
held that his attempt to subvert it was a solitary protest.[5]
It might well survive his proposed amendment, which
is equally untenable, serving as it does merely to force

[1] Work cited, ch. ix.   [2] *Id.* p. 30.   [3] *Id.* p. 28.
[4] He quotes Furnivall (p. 62) as putting the strong proposition that
for Hamlet the murder of his father is " only a skin-deep stain " in comparison with his mother's guilt.
[5] *Id.* p. 5.

into new prominence the fact that the play cannot be explained *from within*.

A similar criticism is elicited by the more studious performance of Professor W. F. Trench, who, though he does not cite them, virtually adopts the formula of Schlegel and Coleridge and Lowell, accounting for Hamlet's non-performance by representing him as a man of con-templation, reacting only mentally, being from the first incapable of the required action.[1] The thesis seems unnecessarily complicated, not to say confused, by the further position that Hamlet is chronically " pretty mad "[2]—a theory which pretty well dispenses with the psychological analysis to which the writer devotes so much ability. The play is thus at once a " tragedy of inefficiency,"[3] of " the will-less-ness proper to the contemplative genius,"[4] and of a virtual insanity which is equally proper to that genius. We are therefore not to be surprised if we cannot understand Hamlet : " he cannot understand himself "[5]—a proposition surely no less applicable to half the characters in the play—or in any play. But at the same time " We find it hard, with Shakespeare's help, to understand Hamlet : even Shakespeare, perhaps, found it hard to understand him." Perhaps !

And when the critic, after denying that Hamlet can act, dismisses the slaying of Polonius with the remark[6] that " About this ' rash and bloody deed ' Hamlet is *insanely* unconcerned "—adding a footnote insisting that

---

[1] Work cited, pp. 74–9, 119, 137.
[2] Pp. 76, 86–7, 107, 131, 161, 163, 227.
[3] P. 172.   [4] P. 119, *note.*
[5] P. 143. On p. 138 we have : " It must be admitted that Hamlet did not *always* correctly analyse his own motives."
[6] P. 173.

his " I took thee for thy better " is only an afterthought
—and again dismisses the doom of Rosencrantz and
Guildenstern with the comment : [1] " A bloody thought
enabling him to write a letter that will lead to their
destruction," we seem entitled to doubt whether the
critic understands Hamlet either ; whether, in fact, this
whole business of " understanding Hamlet " is not a
following of a will-o'-the-wisp, to be renounced in favour
of the task of " understanding HAMLET." The light
from within invariably resolving itself into a multiplicity
of shifting lights, we are compelled to seek light from
without.

§ 4. The Growth of the Play.

The history of the play is thus vital to the compre-
hension of it. A real life is the life of an organism ; and
a biography, whether general or episodic, is a necessarily
imperfect and selective presentment of .a life by way
of narrative, document, and explanation. Its final value
is in proportion to the vividness and the consistency
with which it presents the organic personality, whether
that be consistent or inconsistent, *recognizing* the latter
quality where it subsists. A fiction is a willed *mechanism*,
simulating under an artistic form the presentment of
the career of an organism ; and its artistic validity is
finally in terms of its measure of simulative success.
Now, though the author of a fiction may use the device
of pretended doubt as to the motives of his characters
by way of heightening illusion on one side, that device
is proper only to the novel, which admits of commentary.
A play does not ; and it is not rightly the business of

[1] P. 224.

a dramatist to leave a character unintelligible. In the words of Gildon, he is " master of the story " : that is, he ought to be. So obvious is this that when the failure happens we are entitled to infer either (a) oversight or confusion on the part of the dramatist, or (b) some difficulty imposed by his material.[1] And it is easy to show that, while Shakespeare is certainly capable of oversight and of occasional confusion, in this case he has suffered or accepted a compulsion imposed by material which, as a stage-manager revising a popular play of marked action, he did not care to reject.

In a word, the dramatist is conditioned on the one hand by his qualities, congenital and acquired, and on the other hand by his matter ; and when the matter emerges as a prior play, with striking situations which constitute its " drawing " power, the conditioning on that side is apt to be constringent. Professor Bradley sees and states with perfect clearness and fulness the probable play of the personal equation in Shakespeare, the effects or limitations of culture, pressure of time, fatigue over an uncongenial task, knowledge of the low standards and poor taste of the bulk of his audience, and so on.[2] But in HAMLET, the first of the great plays in which Shakespeare fully reveals his supremacy, there is far more evidence of superabundant power and of keen interest in the main theme than of haste or carelessness —apart from his habitual indifference to time measurement. When then the play falls short of intelligibility in itself, it is at once the economical and the necessary course to look for the solution in the conditions imposed

---

[1] Professor Bradley, who expressed himself more uncompromisingly (as cited above, p. 24, *note*) would presumably assent to this.
[2] *Shakespearean Tragedy*, 2nd ed. p. 75.

by the material. Without a study of these we are very much in the position of the geocentric astronomer, revolving in an incomplete induction. The history of the play alone elucidates the main issue.

II

THE DOCUMENTARY PROBLEM

§ 1. The Pre-Shakespearean Play.

MOST critics have long been agreed that there was a pre-Shakespearean HAMLET, PRINCE OF DENMARK—presumably that noted by Henslowe as played in 1594—and that its author was Thomas Kyd.[1] Nashe's allusions, in his address " To the Gentleman Students " prefaced to Greene's MENAPHON (1589), concerning " shifting companions that run through every art and thrive by none," leaving " the trade of *Noverint* whereto they were born " ; " whole *Hamlets*, I should say handfuls, of tragical speeches " ; " Seneca let blood line by line and page by page," " the Kid in Æsop " ; " Italian translations," and " twopenny pamphlets," point clearly and solely to Thomas Kyd.   He was the son of a scrivener ; he is known to have issued at least one pamphlet, which is preserved, and to have translated Tasso's treatise on household management (1588), and he echoes Seneca throughout his SPANISH TRAGEDY.   The earlier theory that " trade of *Noverint* " pointed to Shakespeare is ruled out alike by date and by biographical fact.   The identi-

---

[1] The hypothesis was first put by Malone.

3

fication of Kyd, definitely begun by English writers,[1] has been carried further by Herr Gregor Sarrazin in his THOMAS KYD UND SEIN KREIS (Berlin, 1892), where actual survivals of Kyd's phraseology in HAMLET, especially in the First Quarto, are specified:

Bellimperia.   Farewell, my lord,
          Be mindful of my love and of your word.
Andrea.   'Tis fixed upon my heart.
                     First Part of Jeronymo : Dodsley's Old Plays,
                     2nd ed., iii. 70.[2]
Learles.   Farewell, Ophelia, and remember well what I have
                     said to you.
Ophelia.   It is already lock't within my heart.
                                 Hamlet, 1st Q. Rep., 1860, p. 16.

          Fair locks, resembling Phœbus' radiant beams,
          Smooth forehead, like the table of high Jove.
                                 Soliman and Perseda, 333.
          Hyperion's curls ; the front of Jove himself.
                                 Hamlet, Fol. III, iv. 56.

          Importing health and wealth of Soliman.
                                 S. and P. V, i. 24.
          Importing Denmark's health and England's too.
                                 Hamlet, V. ii.

Isabella.   O where's the author of this *endless woe ?*
Hieronimo.   To know the author were some ease of grief,
          For in *revenge* my *heart* would find *relief.*
                                 Spanish Tragedy, II. v. 39.
          Revenge it is must yield my *heart relief,*
          For *woe begets woe,* and grief hangs on grief.
                                 Hamlet, 1st Q. Rep. cited, p. 83.

---

[1] *E.g.* W. H. Widgery, *Harness Prize Essays on the First Quarto,* 1880, p. 100 sq. One of Sarrazin's parallels, given below, is indicated by Widgery, p. 160.

[2] This play is not Kyd's, but founded on his *Comedy of Don Horatio.* See below, p. 53 sq.

Bellimperia.	Hieronimo, I will *consent, conceal,*
	And aught that may effect for thine avail,
	Join with thee to revenge Horatio's death.
Hieronimo.	On, then ; and *whatsoever I devise,*
	Let me entreat you, grace my practices.

S.T. IV. i. 45 (V. 146).

| *Gertrude.* | I will *consent, conceal,* and do my best, |
| | *What* stratagem *soe'er thou shalt devise.* |

Hamlet, 1st Q. Rep. cited, p. 65.

The parallels to " Hyperion's curls " and " Importing health " may be challenged on the ground that the First Quarto does not yield them ; but as regards the last two there can be no rebuttal. The Quarto lines disappear in the Second Quarto and the Folio ; and they are plainly Kyd's. Further, though the First Quarto certainly consists mainly of Shakespeare matter, some of it greatly mangled, some not, it has many passages which are plainly non-Shakespearean. Professor Dowden, adhering to a position taken up in the past by various critics, including Grant White and the German Mommsen, committed himself to the declaration :

> For my own part, repeated perusals have satisfied me that Shakespeare's hand can be discerned throughout the whole of the truncated and travestied play of 1603. . . . With the exception of the following lines :
>> Look you now, here is your husband,
>> With a face like Vulcan,
>> A look fit for a murder and a rape,
>> A dull dead hanging look, and a hell-bred eye
>> To affright children and amaze the world,
>
> I see nothing that looks pre-Shakespearean, and I see much that is entirely unlike the work of Kyd.[1]

But the first and last propositions are beside the case, since no one denies that there is a great deal of Shake-

---

[1] Introd. to *Hamlet* in " Arden " ed., p. xviii.

speare in the Quarto ; and the other denial was surely an oversight. The " revenge " lines and the " consent, conceal " lines, just cited, and seen by the Professor in Sarrazin, *are* pre-Shakespearean ; and in a dozen places we have a plainly pre-Shakespearean basis for passages which Shakespeare rewrote. Take Ophelia's reply to Laertes :

> Brother, to this I have lent attentive ear,
> And doubt not but to keep my honour firm ;
> But, my dear brother, do not you,
> Like to a cunning sophister,
> Teach me the path and ready way to heaven,
> While you, forgetting what is said to me,
> Yourself, like to a careless libertine,
> Doth give his heart, his appetite at full,
> And little recks how that his honour dies.

This is not a misreporting of the speech given us in the Second Quarto : it is a transcript, probably imperfect in two lines, of a speech in a feebler and flatter style and versification. Similarly Ophelia's account to her father of Hamlet's distraction begins in the First Quarto in a non-Shakespearean style :

> O young Prince Hamlet, the only flower of Denmark,
> He is bereft of all the wealth he had ;
> The jewel that adorn'd his features most
> Is filcht and stol'n away ; his wit's bereft him ;

as does the speech of Polonius to the king and queen, telling how he had ordered Ophelia to refuse the Prince's addresses. It is earlier and poorer matter,[1] which in

---

[1] Mr. Widgery, in his brilliant prize essay (*Harness Prize Essays*, 1880), finds Shakespearean quality in these passages. I cannot. Professor Herford (essay in same vol., p. 84) partly leans to Mr. Widgery at this point, but notes non-Shakespearean matter.

the Second Quarto is rewritten. The version of the
" To be " soliloquy in the first may possibly be only a
mangling of what we have in the second ; but this cannot
be said of the king's soliloquy in the prayer scene :

> O that this wet that falls upon my face
> Would wash the crime clear from my conscience !
> When I look up to heaven, I see my trespass ;
> The earth doth still cry out upon my fact,
> [Pay me ?] the murder of a brother and a king ;
> And the adulterous fault I have committed :
> O these are sins that are unpardonable.
> Why, say thy sins were blacker than is jet,
> Yet may contrition make them white as snow.
> Aye, but still to persever in a sin
> Is an act 'gainst the universal power.
> Most wretched man, stoop, bend thee to thy prayer ;
> Ask grace of heaven to keep thee from despair.

This is not a first draft by Shakespeare, any more than
it is a misreport of the soliloquy of the Second Quarto :
it is pre-Shakespearean. And these and other equally
non-Shakespearean passages are printed by Professor
Dowden in an Appendix, with no suggestion there that
they are unlike the manner of Kyd. They are in fact
quite in the manner of THE SPANISH TRAGEDY and ARDEN
OF FEVERSHAM.[1]

But we have further the phraseological clues given by
Widgery and Sarrazin, to which may be added these :

1. In the scene between Horatio and the Queen after
Hamlet's return, which appears only in the First Quarto,
we have the line :

> For murderous minds are always jealous,

---

[1] Kyd's authorship of *Arden*, first contended for by Fleay, and sup-
ported by the present writer in *Did Shakespeare write ' Titus Andronicus ' ?*
has been independently and conclusively established by Mr. Charles
Crawford (*Collectanea*, vol. i).

where *jealous* must be read as a trisyllable, *jelious*. The word is so scanned in the SPANISH TRAGEDY (II. ii. 56), and its occurrence with that scansion four times in ARDEN is one of the many clues to Kyd's authorship of that play. All four lines chime exactly with that cited.

2. The revenge-grief couplet quoted by Sarrazin from the First Quarto follows a line which also is an echo of Kyd, by himself:

> Therefore I will not *drown thee* in *my tears*.

Compare:

> To *drown thee* with an ocean of *my tears*.
> *Spanish Tragedy*, II. v. 23.

3. " As raging as the sea," in the Queen's speech to the King after the closet scene, is but a slight clue (*S.T.* IV. iii. 101); but in the line:

> He might be once tasked *for to try your cunning*,

in the First Quarto's version of the King's talk to Leartes after learning of Hamlet's return—a piece of dialogue clearly pre-Shakespearean—the " for to " points to Kyd, who uses that idiom eight times in ARDEN. The " for to " in the line:

> For to adorn a king and guild his crown,

in the First Quarto's closet scene, is probably a misprint for " fit to."

4. But there emerges here a further clue, noted by Professor Boas,[1] which clinches the other.   In the SPANISH TRAGEDY Bellimperia says (IV. i. 178) :

You mean to *try my cunning*, then, Hieronimo.

These small coincidences become progressively significant as they accumulate ; and Professor Boas has noted yet others.

5. After the King in the First Quarto has remarked to Leartes : " He might be once tasked for to try your cunning," Leartes asks :

And how for this ?

and the King begins his reply :

Marry, Leartes, thus.

Exactly in the same fashion, in the TRAGEDY, when Hieronimo has been talking to Lorenzo of tragedy-writing, the latter asks (IV. i. 74) :

And how for that ?

and Hieronimo replies :

Marry, my good Lord, thus.

And in both cases the explanation given is met in the same way, Leartes saying, " 'Tis excellent," and Lorenzo, " O excellent."

[1] Introd. to Kyd's works, 1901, p. li.

6. Yet again, there is a close parallel of phrase and situation between the feigned reconciliation of Leartes and Hamlet in the First Quarto and that of Castile's son and Hieronimo in the TRAGEDY (III. xiv. 154). The King says to Gertrude:

> We'll have Leartes and our son
> Make friends and lovers as befits them both.

Castile says:

> But here, before Prince Balthazar and me,
> Embrace each other, and be perfect friends.

In both cases, as Professor Boas points out, the formal reconciliation is the prelude to the catastrophe.

7. Another echo noted by Professor Boas and others occurs in connection with the play scenes. Hamlet in the First Quarto (III. ii.) cries:

> And if the King like not the tragedy,
> Why then, belike, he likes it not, perdy.

So Hieronimo in the TRAGEDY (IV. i. 196–7):

> And if the world like not this Tragedy,
> Hard is the hap of old Hieronimo.

8. And yet again we have the cry of Hamlet:

> I never gave you cause,

echoed in that of Lorenzo (*S.T.*, III. xiv. 148):

> Hieronimo, I never gave you cause.

To refuse to see in this string of verbal coincidences a proof of the survival of portions of Kyd's original text in HAMLET is to evade phenomena which can be explained in no other way. They set up the same problem as we are faced-by in the multitude of echoes from Peele in TITUS ANDRONICUS. If we are to suppose Shakespeare in these cases composing a play of his own, we conceive him as parroting in the weakest way two of his contemporaries who were incomparably his inferiors in literary power. A tag or a poetic trope he might and did echo from other poets, as they so constantly echoed each other ; but here we have many phrases which are not current tags, and tropes not worth repeating. If Shakespeare penned them he was simply copying other men's humdrum dialogue, as if for lack of power to make his own independently. The conception only needs to be put clearly in order to be rejected. The young Shakespeare was not more but less likely than other men to plagiarize thus weakly and slothfully. In KING JOHN, as later in LEAR, he rewrites a whole play without copying a line.

Seeing, then, that in the parts of our play under notice there is no question of the intervention of any other hand, we are bound in candour and in common-sense, having regard to all the other cogent evidence for Kyd's origination of HAMLET, to decide that the score of echoes above noted signify the survival of so much of his matter in Shakespeare's first adaptation. In the relatively small quantity of clearly non-Shakespearean work detachable from the First Quarto, the number of the echoes is conclusive.

§ 2. The Old German Version.

But the really important problem is not so much to detach survivals of Kyd's phraseology in HAMLET as to ascertain with some precision what is of his determination in the structure and action of the play. We know from the early allusions that his Hamlet played the madman and cried " Revenge," and that the old play had a Ghost. So much might have been inferred from a comparison of the machinery in the existing play and the SPANISH TRAGEDY ; and we might confidently infer that Kyd had introduced the play-within-the-play, and also the Dumb Show. As confidently might we expect him to delay the revenge of Hamlet in some such fashion as he delays that of Hieronimo ; and to effect a similarly comprehensive catastrophe. Even the suicide of Ophelia duplicates that of Isabella.

But actions having a general resemblance might be handled very differently in detail, and to ascertain as closely as may be Kyd's actual procedure we must examine the old German play DER BESTRAFTE BRUDER-MORD, otherwise TRAGEDY OF HAMLET, PRINCE OF DENMARK, probably identical with the tragedy of " Hamlet, Prince of Denmark " known to have been played, with many other Elizabethan pieces, at the Court of Dresden in 1626.[1] This, though preserved only through a manuscript of 1710, is at bottom clearly an early form of our HAMLET.[2] Like the First Quarto, it has the name Corambis (Corambus in the German

---

[1] Cohn, *Shakespeare in Germany*, 1865, p. cxv. sq.

[2] Latham, in his *Two Dissertations* (1872) suggested that the German play may have been the original, and that the English travelling players may have brought the account of it home with them. This will not old for an instant.

play) for Polonius; and though the dialogue is visibly much retrenched, it apparently represents an earlier state of the play than that version. It possesses also a Prologue in which Night is the principal speaker, assisted by Alecto, Mægera and Tisiphone—in all probability a rendering of a prologue by Kyd.[1] Professor Dowden, demurring to the use of this play by Mr. John Corbin as evidence for his thesis[2] that the early Hamlet and Ophelia were turned to partly comic purpose, and that Hamlet was substantially a man of action, puts it as "far more probable that the German play is a debased adaptation of Shakespeare's HAMLET in its earliest form."[3] But that thesis really does not exclude that which it repugns, seeing that Dowden accepted Kyd's authorship of the 1589 HAMLET, and does not suggest that Shakespeare's is a wholly new construction. Granting as he does the origination, it is difficult to see why he should have doubted that the simpler conception of the hero seen in the German play points back to Kyd. It seems probable indeed that the primitive episode in which the German Hamlet contrives that the two ruffians commissioned to kill him (in place of Rosencrantz and Guildenstern) shall shoot each other when they mean to shoot him, is a substitution for Hamlet's narrative of the altered letter, which could not be staged. The story of the altered letter is in Belleforest's tale of Amleth, and so lay to Kyd's hand. But not only is the prologue markedly in the taste of Kyd's Ghost and Revenge epilogues in the SPANISH TRAGEDY and those of Love, Fortune and Death in SOLIMAN; the simpler action

---

[1] Cp. Widgery, as cited, p. 105. This is the answer to Latham's point that the German prologue suggests a German poet of some power.
[2] *The Elizabethan Hamlet*, 1895.   [3] Introd. cited, p. xiv.

of Hamlet is precisely what we should expect from him.

By Dowden's admission, there was a Ghost in the Kyd play : it is testified to in Lodge's allusion in WITS MISERIE in 1596 ; and there was a play-within-the-play in that piece as in the SPANISH TRAGEDY. The play-within-the-play in the First Quarto differs in diction and in character-names from that in the Second ; and is clearly primitive.[1] What kind of action, then, and what kind of psychology, was Kyd likely to put in his piece ? We should expect from him a delayed revenge, as in the TRAGEDY, but a revenge delayed simply—or partly—through lack of opportunity or fear of miscarriage, as in that case. Now, in the BRUDERMORD, Hamlet tells Horatio immediately after the Ghost scene what he has learned, and explains that he proposes to feign madness. That Hamlet *had* so enlightened Horatio is indicated in our HAMLET (III. ii. 81) as in the First Quarto, though the scene of the communication has disappeared in the process of transmutation which creates the mystery of the play. There is no hint of the kind of difficulty formulated by Klein and Werder—the impossibility of proving the king's guilt by citing the statement of the Ghost. Hamlet in the German play makes use of the visit of the players as in our play, but he writes nothing for them : he simply commands them to play the play of " King Pyrrhus," whose brother pours juice of hebenon in his ears as in our drama. The German Hamlet, like the English, is quite satisfied with the result, and he shows no paralysing melancholy. He is, in short, as much a man of action as Jeronymo, delaying only because

[1] On p. 180 of his Prize Essay, Mr. Widgery seems to assign the idea to Shakespeare ; but on p. 204 he admits that it was in the " Ur-Hamlet."

he must, though the delay is as it were artistically elaborated.

Before the advent of the players he explains to Horatio (II. v.) :

> By this pretended madness I hope to find opportunity to avenge my father's death.   But you know my father [1] [*i.e.* the present King] *is always surrounded by many guards,* so that I may chance to miscarry, and you may find my dead body.   Let it then be honourably buried, for on the first opportunity I find I will try to kill him.

Then, when Horatio suggests that the Ghost may be a deceiver, the actors arrive ; and although Hamlet has no doubts, he sets his trap by their means.   It is all in Kyd's way of episodically developing and prolonging an action.

Equally simple has been Hamlet's action towards Ophelia, in which there is neither passion nor pathos. With her, he plays the pseudo-madman comically, not tragically, and his " get thee to a nunnery " is a ribaldry. All the same, his method in his madness arouses the suspicions of the King, as in our play, only Corambus and Ophelia being deluded, as in that.   After the play scene, as in our tragedy, Hamlet has the chance to kill the praying King, and abstains, for the theological reason, with this noteworthy difference, that he bethinks him that to kill the praying person is to " take his sins upon thee."   Then he goes to the Queen, seeking an audience, not sent for, and proceeds to reproach her, making reference to the pictures, as in our play.   Corambus is hidden, as there, and is killed in the same fashion ; whereupon

[1] In the First Quarto, Hamlet twice addresses the King as " father." Rep. cited, pp. 50, 68 (at III. ii. 100, and IV. iii. 32).   The word disappears in Q. 2 and Folio.

immediately the Ghost appears, with thunder and lightning, invisible and inaudible to the Queen. Hamlet
takes the visitation simply as a demand for the hastening
of his vengeance : there is no dialogue, and no real self-
reproach, any more than there is any sense of real guilt
on the part of Jeronymo when Bellimperia denounces
his delay. The delay in each case is for Kyd simply
the necessary involution of the drama. There is no
intentional mystery about his Hamlet.

Laertes (Leonhardus) in the German version returns
to avenge his father, and is pacified by the King, as in
our play : the main action is all given. The King, however, plans the poisoned foil as in the First Quarto,
Laertes doubtfully assenting. There is no burial of
Ophelia. She has gone mad, in a fashion to entertain
the groundlings. Here, perhaps, there has been a German
vulgarization, for Kyd had the tragic sense ; but the
German Phantasmo, to whom the mad Ophelia attaches
herself, reveals the basis of Osric. Hamlet has paid no
further heed to Ophelia ; and when at the outset of the
fencing scene the Queen brings the news of her suicide,
the fencing goes on without a pause ! Here again there
has probably been compression.

At the beginning of the fifth Act Hamlet is simply
concerned because his vengeance is still delayed, the
fratricide being " always surrounded by so many people."
" But I swear," he adds, " that ere the sun has made
his journey from the East to the West, I will revenge
myself on him." Then he tells Horatio of his experiences
(there is no graveyard scene), and is interrupted by the
arrival of Phantasmo with the invitation to the fencing
match. Hamlet fools with Phantasmo in the fashion
in which in our play he fools with Polonius ; but immedi-

ately afterwards is struck with apprehension and faints with terror because his nose bleeds. He accordingly goes to Court with a foreboding, and the fencing takes place as in our play, with the difference that the news of Ophelia's suicide is interjected as aforesaid, at the outset.

The changing of the foils, the wounding and confession of Leonhardus, the King's proffer of the poisoned drink, the Queen's interception of it, her death, and Hamlet's stabbing of the King, all follow in due course. But there is no glad acceptance of death on the part of Hamlet, who tells Horatio that his soul is now at peace, seeing that he is revenged; and that he hopes his wound will amount to nothing. In his lament for his mother, who has "half earned this death through her sins," he inquires who gave her the poisoned drink, and, learning that it was Phantasmo, stabs him. Then the poison o'ercrows his spirit, and with his dying breath he tells Horatio to carry the crown to Norway to " my cousin, Duke Fortempras, so that the kingdom may not fall into other hands. Oh, alas, I die." And Horatio winds up with a brief discourse, ending with four lines of sententious verse. There has been no previous mention of Fortempras, which again is doubtless a result of curtailment, as the entire German play is not half the length of the SPANISH TRAGEDY.

And here we are led to face a problem that seems to have been ignored by all save one hostile critic of HAMLET, that, namely, of the superfluous matter in the structure as it stands. The German play has the distinction of eliminating a quantity of detail that in no way helps the central action, reducing that to comparative simplicity and unity. There is thus a presumption that the existing version is the result of successive compressions. HAMLET is the longest of all the Shakespeare plays, having 3,931 lines to the 3,332 of the long LEAR ; yet the BRUDERMORD is the shortest of the three principal German versions of Shakespeare tragedies reproduced by Cohn—considerably shorter than the TITUS ANDRONICUS, and much shorter than the ROMEO AND JULIET. There is, in fact, more removable matter in HAMLET than in any other of the plays named. How then came it to be present ?

III

KYD'S PROBABLE CONSTRUCTION

§ 1. Superfluous Survivals.

So many admiring critics have pronounced HAMLET a gravely faulty play that it is unnecessary to labour the general proposition. Seldom, however, has the verdict been accompanied by a careful analysis; and that is now our business.

In 1873 the German poet Benedix, in his work DIE SHAKSPEREOMANIE, carrying on the debate on that theme which began in Germany with the tercentenary of 1864, contended that HAMLET is ill-constructed in respect of five episodes which have only the effect of hampering the action:

(1) The despatch and return of the embassy to Norway have not the slightest interest for us. But weeks or months [1] must pass before the embassy returns.

(2 and 3) The journey of Laertes to Paris, and the sending of Reynaldo after him, are equally irrelevant. The directions of Polonius to Reynaldo have no interest for us, and we are left waiting for his return, which cannot take place for weeks or months.

(4) The journey of Fortinbras through Denmark to

---

[1] This seems excessive. A few weeks would suffice.

Poland, involving the use of ships, must take months, and for his return also we are kept waiting.

(5) Hamlet's journey to England puts off the dénoûment just when the action is heightening, and leaves us again waiting.

"We thus see," sums up Benedix, "four persons travel away out of the piece ; and not till late do they come back again. These journeys are wholly superfluous episodes. They cause the time of the action to be extended many months ; and it is due to these episodes, and to them alone, that Hamlet's slowness becomes such a mystery. The fourth Act looks like an interpolation introduced in the previous play." [1]

If we take up the position which seems implicit in Professor Bradley's method of interpretation, that Shake-speare's *use* of the prior material is to be considered his *plan*, such criticism as the above, in so far as it may be valid, tells for us not only against the play but against the playwright ; and it is a pity that Professor Dowden should have thought fit to dismiss the criticism of Benedix as merely trivial.[2] It is not trivial ; and if Shakespeare is to be justified in the traditional manner it must be faced.[3] Even if it be claimed that Hamlet's dismissal to England is part of the original saga, and is rightly to be embodied as part of his " weird," there arises the demurrer that the playwright has altered the saga by arresting Hamlet's voyage and bringing him back, thus merely lengthening the action without any effect on the sequel. As for the episodes of the embassies, the mission of Reynaldo, and the campaign of Fortinbras, they are

[1] Furness's Variorum *Hamlet*, ii. 351.
[2] *Shakspere Primer*, p. 165.
[3] Professor Trench in his " Commentary " (p. 49) not only says nothing of the irrelevance of the embassy in Act I. sc. ii., he comments : " And now to business."

visibly excrescences on the plot as they stand, seeing that even the impression made by the expedition on Hamlet, rousing him to a fresh vow of immediate action, does not produce such action, the dismissal to England supervening all the same.

But that the fourth Act was framed as a whole by Shakespeare merely to make out the five is a weak and false hypothesis. The play is far too long for stage purposes ; the first Act could easily have been divided into two at the fourth scene, where we have a new and important action ;[1] and the fourth Act contains the necessary plot for the fencing scene. It was, moreover, certainly given in the main to Shakespeare by his original.

As regards the embassy, the mission of Reynaldo, and the expedition of Fortinbras, the case is different. These are in no way necessary, as the play stands, to the final action ; and, for that very reason, to suppose that Shakespeare invented them is to impute to him a kind of gratuitous mismanagement impossible to him as a practical playwright. Rather we must assume that they too were given him ; and pronounce that his error lay in retaining them. The Reynaldo scene is either a retention of a previous scene that is practically superseded by the actual introduction of Laertes, or an attempt at a *genre* effect such as we find so often in Chapman and Jonson. The disappearance from the German play of all the scenes named is a result of the recognition of their superfluity either by the original English actors who took the play to Germany or by some later German adapters.

---

[1] See below, p. 56, as to the cessation of the numbering of Acts and scenes in the Folio after II. ii. It is generally agreed that Act IV has been wrongly divided, its earlier scenes belonging to Act III.

That the episodes of the embassy and the expedition were given by Kyd is the hypothesis forced upon us by a study of the structure of the play in comparison with that of the SPANISH TRAGEDY. That the mission of Reynaldo was given by Kyd is more.doubtful, though we have it in the First Quarto, with the name Montano instead of Reynaldo. If it be not Kyd's, it is still presumably pre-Shakespearean : that is to say, it is highly unlikely that Shakespeare was the first to load the play with such an irrelevance as it finally amounts to. But it is just possible that in an earlier form of the play Reynaldo's mission counted for something in the action, even as there is reason to think that the embassy and the expedition of Fortinbras had a part in an original action still more multifarious than the present.

An obvious objection to such a suggestion is· that for any more widespread action there was simply no room, unless we suppose that much of the dialogue in the existing play was wholly unrepresented in the original. But I do not propose to employ this rebuttal : there is an alternative explanation.

§ 2. Was Kyd's "Hamlet" a Double Play?

Over twenty years ago I tentatively put forward the hypothesis that HAMLET as we have it may be a condensation of a double play. The suggestion, so far as I know, met with no discussion ; and I have not till now repeated it ; but to-day, on a fresh survey of the problem, it still seems to me a possible solution of the evaded problem. Three circumstances should be noted before it is discussed on its merits :

I. About the time of the publication of HAMLET,

Shakespeare was concerned in the reduction of Whetstone's two-part play of PROMOS AND CASSANDRA to a single play, MEASURE FOR MEASURE.

2. There were current a number of sequel-plays ; [1] and there is strong reason for thinking, with Fleay, that JULIUS CÆSAR as it stands is a compression of two plays into one.

3. Kyd's SPANISH TRAGEDY is a member of a double play. Henslowe enters a *Spanes* (*Spanish*) *comodye donne oracoe* in February 1592, and this is repeatedly played on a day before *Jeronymo*—the old name for the SPANISH TRAGEDY.

It cannot have been the existing FIRST PART OF JERONIMO, printed in 1605. The old COMEDY was probably not new in 1592. It is the fourth play named in the Diary, which at this point appears to continue a previous record, now lost. Written before 1592, it could not have had such a number of double endings as the existing FIRST PART, which has forty-four in the first Act, as against only a dozen in the whole TRAGEDY. The FIRST PART being further in the main markedly different in style from Kyd's work, Mr. Greg and Professor Boas agree that it is much later (*circa* 1600 ?), adding that it is not a comedy.[2] As to this I would make a demur. The original play must, like this, have included the death of Don Andrea, by way of preluding the TRAGEDY, yet it was called a comedy ; and there are many instances in which serious drama was in those

---

[1] On the French stage of the period, sequences sometimes ran for as many as eight days—an outcome of the old practice in "mystery-plays." The fullest extension of sequence on the Tudor stage occurred in the case of the Chronicle plays, which would give the cue to sequels in general drama. Chapman has thus two double-plays in the next decade.

[2] *Henslowe's Diary*, ed. Greg, ii. 150.

days styled "comical." [1]   Deaths did not necessarily make a tragedy, provided that the hero was successful, and Horatio is so in the FIRST PART.   That play, then, is presumably a rewriting of the old COMEDY OF DON HORATIO, preserving its main action, and probably parts of its text ; and we are left with the presumption that Kyd wrote the COMEDY, whether before or after JERONIMO it is impossible to guess.

On the whole it seems to have been much less successful than the TRAGEDY, for while we have in Henslowe several sequences of "doneoracio" and "Jeronymo," the latter is far more frequently played by itself throughout 1592.   It was played by Lord Strange's men, and does not appear in the repertory of the Earl of Sussex's company in 1593–4, or in those of the combinations of the Queen's men and Sussex's, or the Admiral's men and the Lord Chamberlain's, in the same years.   Not till 1597 does JERONYMO reappear [2] in the Diary ; and the COMEDY never reappears at all, while the other goes on steadily.

Assuming that the FIRST PART proceeds on the main lines of the COMEDY, and that the COMEDY was Kyd's, we may get some light from the former on Kyd's mode of construction.   It starts with an embassy from Spain to Portugal to demand over-due tribute.   A refusal leads to the fighting in which Don Andrea is killed.   Don

---

[1] *E.g. The Comical History of Alphonsus King of Arragon*, by Greene, printed in 1599.

[2] Creizenach (*Gesch des neueren Dramas*, IV. i. 539) notes that "Jeronymo" is entered in Henslowe's Diary on 7th January, 1597, as "ne" (new), and, taking the reference to be to the *First Part*, pronounces that the priority of the *Tragedy* [now generally admitted] is thus proved. But the reference is probably to a mere reproduction of the *Tragedy* with some new matter.   "Ne" frequently means this in Henslowe. If it were the *First Part* he would have called it so.   "Jeronymo" is always his name for the *Tragedy*.

Balthazar, the Portuguese Prince, is hot for refusal, and fights valiantly. He is primarily a counterpart of Fortinbras; and there is ground for a presumption that Kyd would have given the latter more than a merely negative part to play. The "post-haste and romage in the land" described in the first scene of HAMLET is dramatically irrelevant to the present action; and the story of the combat between the fathers of Fortinbras and Hamlet ultimately serves no purpose save to prepare for the succession of Fortinbras at the catastrophe. Was it introduced solely for that purpose? Kyd's method, in the light of his practice, would have been to send the ambassadors to Norway at the outset; and it is quite conceivable that the King's speech at the outset of Scene ii, which we find in the BRUDERMORD beginning almost exactly as it does in our play, but *without* the item of the embassy, was originally the beginning of the piece, *with* that item. It would in fact be properly so placed, chronologically; for the marriage has taken place before the Ghost appears. There has clearly been a rearrangement of scenes and speeches even as between the First and Second Quartos; and the "To be" soliloquy is left ill-placed. It would come properly before the Ghost scene, speaking as it does of "the bourne from which no traveller returns." [1]

The obvious effectiveness of the Ghost scene as an introduction would explain easily its transference to that position, supposing it to have been originally placed later. Kyd's method indeed would presumably have

---

[1] It is even conceivable that this speech, in a pre-Shakespearean form, was originally written for another play. It has no proper place in *Hamlet* after the Ghost scene. It might have held the place of the present soliloquy in I. ii.: "O that this too, too solid flesh would melt"; but that, too, in a prior form, is in the First Quarto.

been to prelude with a Ghost prologue ; and to develop
that into a dramatic scene would be in the obvious course
of theatrical development. As it is, the preparations of
Fortinbras are idly made to explain " this our watch,"
as if there would not be sentinels on the King's castle
at all times. Such rearrangements of play-openings
take place on our own stage in the case of non-literary
pieces. It is to be observed, too, that the scene in which
Hamlet sees the Ghost is not numbered in the Folio,
and that after the second scene of Act II the numbering
of Acts and scenes ceases altogether. Apparently there
has been a rearrangement which upset the original
divisions.[1] As the case stands, Hamlet's scene with the
Ghost, which takes much longer to play than to read,
would make an Act in itself.

One possible clue to the original employment of the
Fortinbras motive is given in the German play, in the
scene in which, before meeting the Ghost, Hamlet tells
Horatio how the King has had himself crowned while
Hamlet was in Germany ; " *but with a show of right he
has made over to me the crown of Norvay,* and appealed
to the election of the States." It seems impossible to
account for this passage as a German invention, since
it in no way concerns the remaining action. It must
surely belong to the pre-Shakespearean play. And the
presumption is that on this pretext Kyd brought his
Hamlet and Fortinbras into some conflict, which not
only filled the stage for a time but prepared for the
bequest of the crown at the close.

As it is, the account of the old combat between the

---

[1] As there is great diversity throughout the Folio as to the numbering
of Acts and scenes, it cannot be specially argued from in the case of
Hamlet ; but probable rearrangements would seem to be the likely
explanation in most of the cases.

kings of Denmark and Norway presents a situation in which the lands of the elder Fortinbras—that is to say, the Kingdom of Norway [1]—had been forfeited to the elder Hamlet, King of Denmark. Such a situation would provide an action lengthening the play to such an extent that the death of Polonius, followed by the dispatch of Hamlet to England, may have been the conclusion of a " First Part," leaving the second to begin with the return of Laertes to seek *his* revenge. And such a break would give the necessary interval for the return of Laertes, which is now lacking.

Such a procedure seems likely enough for Kyd. Duplication seems to have been the note of his early work. In the Kyd HAMLET, a " murdered Ghost " figures as in the TRAGEDY ; a play-within-a-play figures in both ; Fortinbras, as aforesaid, pairs with Balthazar ; Laertes seeks to revenge his father as does Hamlet, merely inverting the order of the TRAGEDY, where the father revenges his son ; Isabella's madness and suicide are duplicated in Ophelia's ; and the suicide of Ophelia in the German play resembles that of Jeronymo. Beginning the second play with the Laertes motive, Kyd might carry on the two themes side by side with the Norwegian complication and the madness of Ophelia.

§ 3. Irrelevant Scenes.

But it would not be in Kyd's way to introduce Laertes without letting us see him informed of his father's death ; and that consideration brings us to the conundrum of the mission of Reynaldo-Montano, which clearly derives

[1] In the old Hamblet story, the combatants are originally not kings but pirate chiefs. Hamblet's father marries the king's daughter.

somehow from a pre-Shakespearean source. That Shakespeare invented such a purposeless episode as the present merely to exhibit the character of Polonius is unthinkable. On the other hand, the scene is not at all in the manner of Kyd. As it stands, it suggests the intervention of another hand between Kyd and Shakespeare, though Shakespeare may have revised.

Such irrelevant scene-writing is the specialty of Chapman, alike in comedy and tragedy. It is abundantly exhibited in MONSIEUR D'OLIVE, where the subsidiary character o'ercrows the plot; and it appears to be Chapman's hand that developed Parolles in ALL'S WELL.[1] As our play now stands, the only conceivable motive for the Reynaldo scene is the theatrical need for comic relief after the tremendous Ghost scene. But if we suppose the mission of Montano-Reynaldo in the original play to have served a purpose in the action, we may guess that in that Montano played the part of a messenger to Laertes with the news of his father's death. On that view we might doubtfully guess that Corambis had been dispatching him on the eve of the play-scene, and that the news of the death, following immediately afterwards and before Montano's departure, replaced the proposed mission. But this is highly problematic; and we can but insist on the obvious probability that the existing scene is neither by Kyd nor by Shakespeare, save in so far as Shakespeare may have recast it.[2] If Kyd had an equivalent scene, it may have stood at the beginning of Act III.

A similar problem arises as to the " To be " soliloquy.

---

[1] See *Shakespeare and Chapman*, pp. 264, 270, 272.
[2] There are twelve double-endings in the first nineteen lines—a *very* high proportion for Shakespeare.

That, as it stands, obviously clashes with the fact of the appearance of the Ghost ; and it is difficult to believe that Kyd had the idea of making Hamlet contemplate suicide immediately after vowing to revenge his father —unless, indeed, by way of crudely shamming madness ; or in a state of partial despair at non - success, like Jeronymo.

In the German play, there is no hint of such a mood ; and in the place where it would have been appropriate in our play—the first Act, *before* the revelation of the Ghost—the ground is already covered by the soliloquy which follows the dialogue of Hamlet with the King and Queen. In the First Quarto, the soliloquy—which here, albeit the text is corrupt, indicates a somewhat different form—follows on Corambis' account to the King and Queen of Hamlet's love-melancholy upon Ophelia's rejection of his suit. The Queen withdraws, and the King listens to the soliloquy and the subsequent dialogue with Ophelia ; the " fishmonger " talk following. In the Second Quarto, as in the Folio, Polonius entreats the King and Queen to go, proposing *another* opportunity for their overhearing such a dialogue ; and we have at once Hamlet's " fishmonger " dialogue with him, followed by the entrance and dialogue of Guildenstern and Rosencrantz, and the advent of the players ; the " To be " soliloquy and its sequel being relegated to the third Act. All this rearrangement cannot have been the work of the piratical editor. It tells of a protracted process of reconstruction.

It is an open question, then, whether the " To be " soliloquy is an early item in Shakespeare's transmutation of Hamlet into a pessimist ; or whether an original speech has been removed by him, recast, from a more appro-

priate place ; or whether it was originated by the hand
or hands that had begun to recast the play before he
took it up. As it stands, the versification appears to
be his in the first form as well as in the second, allowance
being made for the reporter's corruptions.

For the rest, while we may certainly ascribe a play-
within-the-play to Kyd, with some dialogue on the
functions of the players as we have it in the BRUDERMORD,[1]
it is tolerably certain that neither the player's Pyrrhus-
speech nor the existing interlude is by him. The fact
that Hamlet in the German play begins by recalling a
" Pyr-Pyr-something," and that a king Pyrrhus is there
the counterpart of the Albertus of the First Quarto and
the Gonzago of the Second, raises speculation ; but
the player's speech and the interlude as they stand are
not Kyd's. I have elsewhere suggested that both may
be the work of Chapman, and that Hamlet's compli-
mentary account of the play from which the Pyrrhus
speech was taken may thus have been a tribute to the
" rival poet " from Shakespeare. There is the alternative hypothesis [2] that, as it is certainly an imitation
of Marlowe's DIDO, the imitation may have been made
by Shakespeare in order to pay a compliment to Marlowe,
perhaps after his death. But the existing play-scene I
take to be Chapman's work.[3] The absolute echo of
Greene in the opening lines raises the question whether
that poet may here have collaborated with Kyd in the
original play, or added something to it later, as he seems
to have done to some extent in ARDEN. But if so,
Shakespeare or another had ejected Greene's work to

[1] Admittedly parts of the advice to the player in Q. 1 are non-
Shakespearean.

[2] Put by Widgery, as cited, p. 161.

[3] See *Shakespeare and Chapman*, p. 215 sq.

begin with, for the version in the First Quarto differs entirely at the outset from that in the Second, the Greene lines being absent. The solution I would offer is that the interlude as it stands in the First Quarto is substantially Kyd's; that Chapman may have inserted the passage with the line (echoed in his WIDOW'S TEARS) :

None weds the second but she kills the first,

which is a duplication of the thought in the Queen's next lines; and that he later rewrote the scene for the company, echoing Greene's lines after he had revised Greene in ALL'S WELL, where there is a similar passage.[1] I do not agree with Mr. Widgery that the opening lines in the First Quarto version are beyond the power of Kyd: they seem to me quite possible to the Kyd who translated CORNELIA; and they are really not good enough for Shakespeare.

Kyd it certainly was that introduced the madness and suicide of Ophelia, perhaps vulgarizing the madness in part as is done in the BRUDERMORD in the episode with Phantasmo. But it is his hand that gives the King's lines:

Ah, pretty wretch, this is a change indeed :
O June, how swiftly runs our joys away !
Content on earth was never certain bred ;
To-day we laugh and live, to-morrow dead.

These cannot be Shakespeare's. Neither did Shakespeare write the scene between Hamlet and his mother as it stands in the First Quarto. Even Professor Dowden

[1] See *Shakespeare and Chapman*, p. 266. In *Selimus*, which is certainly in the main Greene's, there is yet another use (l. 41) of the formula there sampled,

gave up part; and the remaining lines wholly lack Shakespeare's touch, though their versification is regular. As we have seen, they include a duplication of lines in the SPANISH TRAGEDY. The lines are probably Kyd's down to the end of the scene.

As for the next, in which Fortinbras passes with his troops, it is probable that Hamlet's soliloquy, Second Quarto, which alone motives it, was already written when the First Quarto was issued, but was dropped in the representation as it is dropped in the Folio, for sheer lack of time. But to Kyd, finally, must we attribute the scene, lacking in the Second Quarto, in which Horatio tells the Queen of Hamlet's safe return—an episode which here is very slightly handled, Hamlet having been simply " set ashore " after having altered the King's letter so as to doom the two courtiers. The scene may have been curtailed; but it is certainly non-Shakespearean, and the line:

But murderous minds are always jealous (jelious),

with its peculiar scansion, points definitely to him. The opening speech by Horatio is probably a rewriting of an earlier; it has four double-endings in seven lines, which Kyd would not have produced in 1589; but the writing is not Shakespeare's. The rest is in Kyd's early manner. Whether he had a graveyard scene it is impossible to guess; but Ben Jonson's phrase, " sporting Kyd," suggests that he did some humourous work; and in the rest of his preserved matter we have none save the Basilisco scenes in SOLIMAN AND PERSEDA, scenes which cannot quite confidently be assigned to him. He may then have introduced a graveyard scene by way of carrying on Hamlet's pretence of madness, which never amounts to much in his hands, so far as the writing goes in the First Quarto and the BRUDERMORD. The probability is that his Hamlet, like the Hamblet of the story, indulged in mad action, to eke out a pretence that was inadequate in respect of the dialogue.

One thing should here be incidentally noted. The association of Horatio with the Queen at the first entrance of Ophelia, in the Second Quarto, is probably due to the simple fact that, Polonius being dead and the missioners gone, there is no other known courtier to introduce. But the arrangement works ill; for Horatio thus knows of Ophelia's madness, yet tells Hamlet nothing of it before the funeral scene. There was no careful reconstruction here.

IV

SHAKESPEARE'S WORK OF TRANSMUTATION

§ 1. Old Action: New Psychosis.

It remains to note how Shakespeare's handling has turned a Hamlet who was very little of a mystery into a Hamlet who is very much one. The first step in counter-sense, certainly, was taken by Kyd, when he combined the revelation by the Ghost with the mock-madness of the old story given him in Belleforest. In that, no Ghost is needed, the murder being known to all, though the traitorous brother (Fengon) persuades the people that he killed Hamblet's father (Horvendile) only in defence of Geruth, Hamblet's mother, who is secretly Fengon's paramour. Hamblet's madness, accordingly, is assumed in the manner of the old myth of Brutus and David, to save his life, he feeling sure that otherwise Fengon will slay him. It is not primarily a matter of wild talk but of demented action, though Hamblet proceeds to make "subtill answers" which arouse Fengon's suspicion, leading him to seek to entrap the youth by means of a "fair and beautiful woman" and "certain courtiers." Here we have the germs of Ophelia and Rosencrantz and Guildenstern; and in the foster-brother who puts Hamblet on his guard we have a hint of Horatio.

Another attempt is made by Fengon to entrap Hamblet in a talk with his mother, with a counsellor concealed behind the hangings,[1] and the counsellor is killed by Hamblet in the manner of the play, which here also follows the story. Before the slaying scene, however, Kyd had previously composed the play-within-the-play, which gratuitously reveals to the King Hamlet's ghost-given knowledge of the murder—a fresh confusion of the old plot. In that, the killing of the courtier is followed by Hamblet's dispatch to England; his counterfeiting of the letters, so as to doom the messengers, as in the play; and his manifold English adventures, which the play ignores.

Whereas, then, the barbaric Hamblet shams madness to save his life, Kyd's Hamlet, who shams madness after supernaturally learning of a wholly secret murder, thereby begins at once to endanger his. Apprised by the Ghost, he had no occasion to alter his behaviour: it was his business to behave as before, the King having thus far no designs on him. And the play-within-the-play is another supererogation. Kyd loved to complicate his motives thus. In ARDEN he introduces items of sacrilege and avarice which are dramatically needless, being motived only by the academic principle that he who suffers must have sinned; and he invents two wronged men, one of whom appears merely to curse, doing nothing further in the action. \ By thus confusing the original Hamlet-plot through his favourite Ghost-motive, Kyd, led to retain the mock-madness by his success with the semi-madness of Jeronymo, prepared the divagation

[1] Under straw in Saxo Grammaticus; under a quilt in Belleforest. The hangings appear in the English translation, of which only a copy dated 1608 exists.

which Shakespeare so wonderfully develops. The Ghost-warned Hamlet who shams madness to no purpose grows naturally into the Hamlet who unintelligibly swerves from revenge.

That Kyd's inconsistencies of construction thus inhere in Shakespeare's play is a fact which criticism must sooner or later face. Lowell, rightly arguing that "if you deprive Hamlet of reason there is no truly tragic motive left," confuses his position by accepting the absurd pronouncement of early Victorian "experts" that Hamlet really exhibits in perfection the symptoms of madness, and explains that "if such a man assumed madness, he would play his part perfectly." Then he remembers that the assumed madness is "one of the few points in which Shakespeare keeps close to the old story," and accordingly declares him to have done so with "unerring judgment." Hamlet, that is to say, shams madness merely because he does not know what else to do: "the scheme of simulated insanity is precisely the one he would have been likely to hit upon, because it enabled him to follow his own bent, and to drift with an apparent purpose," and so forth. Then we are to believe that Shakespeare saw in the expedient of the barbarian of the story, a man of action absolutely, "precisely" what would be done by a man of exactly opposite structure. To such shifts does idolatry conduct us.

We shall ultimately do much more for Shakespeare's credit by honestly acknowledging that his Hamlet pretends madness because Kyd's Hamlet did so before; and that in Kyd's Hamlet the device is put out of joint, first by Kyd's own further device of the Ghost's revelation, which cancels the prudential motive of the saga

Hamblet, making Hamlet on the contrary at once arouse the King's suspicion ; and secondly by the device of the play-within-the-play, which is anything but a madman's plan, though Jeronymo gave the precedent. In a word, Hamlet's mock-madness is now ill-motived. Lowell, in his best " high priori " manner, writes that " Voltaire complains that he [Hamlet] goes mad without any sufficient object or result. Perfectly true, and precisely what was most natural for him to do, and, accordingly, precisely what Shakespeare meant that he should do." What Voltaire really said [1] was that " pour ne pas donner d'ombrages à Gertrude, il contrefait le fou pendant toute la pièce "—a jest which incidentally suggests a better motive for Hamlet's mock-madness than any given by the idolaters. As criticism, Voltaire's fling is perfectly just ; and, like some of his other flings it is to be met, not by brazening things out, but by granting that Shakespeare did at times make himself answerable for other men's artistic sins.[2]   He did so when, essaying his immortal task of transmuting the crude play of Kyd into a dramatic marvel, he retained all the archaic machinery while transfiguring all the characters. A marvel his *tour de force* remains ; but no jugglery can do away with the fact that the construction is incoherent, and the hero perforce an enigma, the snare of idolatrous criticism.

It is of no avail to plead, as Mr. Widgery so eloquently does after Werder, that Hamlet in the play has an insuperably difficult task, seeing that he cannot prove the King's guilt by citing the testimony of a ghost. Why

---

[1] *Lettre à messieurs de l'académie française,* 15 auguste, 1776.

[2] *E.g.* the scene between Henry and Catherine in *Henry V,* which Voltaire contemned. Most of his attacks on Shakespeare turn on real blemishes, and they are bracketed with very high praise. The sin of his criticism is its want of final balance.

did he not at the outset tell both Horatio and Marcellus
what the Ghost had told him? They would have
believed, and been believed, readily enough. Given a
Ghost who is credited by the *audience*, why should he
not be credited by the characters? When, again, the
King rushes away in confusion from the play, it is surely
idle to argue, as does Mr. Widgery, that Hamlet has
failed in his object because the King does not *speak*. Is
not his confusion a sufficient proof of his guilt? To
say that the courtiers do not so recognize it is to argue
in a circle. Shakespeare would never have *planned* a
play on such lines and with such a thesis, any more than
he would have invented the prayer-scene and the motive
that there withholds Hamlet.

All these devices, once more, are but the machinery of
Kyd, adapting a barbaric story in which the barbarian
must delay his revenge because he is only one against a
powerful chief, whom the people heartily support, believ-
ing him to have saved the youth's mother from her
husband's violence. It all goes back, possibly, to a sun
myth; but the barbaric tale is fairly coherent. Kyd
needed a tale of delayed vengeance, and for him, though
he makes Hamlet indirectly accuse himself in the closet-
scene with the Ghost,[1] there was no more mystery in
Hamlet's delay than there was in Jeronymo's, or in the
halting and hindered movement of the action in ARDEN,
with the baffled attempts, and the two reconciliations
of the doomed man with his enemy. Kyd's tragedy-
method was not psychological or didactic, with all his
devotion to Seneca: it is one of protracted and long-

---

[1] In Q. 1 the dialogue is clearly in part Kyd's; and in the *Brudermord*
we have the same deprecation of the supposed wrath of the Ghost at
delay.

baffled action; and he of necessity ekes out the time
with incidents and expedients, especially where, as in
HAMLET, he has a plot full of delays given to his hand.

In the closet-scene in the First Quarto, the Ghost says
nothing of an " almost blunted purpose "; that is
Shakespeare's modification. Kyd has no such conception.
His Hamlet says :

> Do you not come your tardy son to chide,
> That I thus long have let revenge slip by ?

but the Ghost replies only :

> Hamlet, I once again appear to thee
> To put thee in remembrance of my death.
> Do not neglect, nor long time put it off,—

going on to urge him to comfort his mother. This is
wholly in the spirit of the SPANISH TRAGEDY, where the
partly unavoidable and partly artificial delay of revenge
is the great preoccupation of the distracted Jeronymo,
who delays in order to obtain a grand finale of slaughter
by means of his play-within-the-play. He begins plotting
immediately after the murder :

> Meanwhile, good Isabella, cease thy plaints,
> Or at the least dissemble them awhile :
> So shall we sooner find the practice out.
>
> II. v. 113.

When he gets Bellimperia's letter he is suspicious :

> Hieronimo, beware,—thou art betrayed.
> And to entrap thy life this train is laid.
> Advise thee, therefore, be not credulous. . .
> Dear was the life of my beloved son,

And of his death behoves me be reveng'd :
Then hazard not thine own, Hieronimo,
But live t' effect thy resolution
I therefore will by circumstances try
What I can gather to confirm this writ. . . .

                                        III. ii. 37–49.

He contemplates suicide and refrains :

For if I hang or kill myself, let's know
Who will revenge Horatio's murther then ?

He thinks of appealing to the King, but decides to " go
by, go by." He

                    will revenge his [Horatio's] death,
But how ? not as the vulgar wits of men,
With open but inevitable ills,
As by a secret yet a certain mean,
Which under friendship will be cloakèd best.
Wise men will take their opportunity
Closely and safely, fitting things to time ;
But in extremes advantage hath no time ;
And therefore all times fit not for revenge.
Thus therefore will I rest me in unrest,
Dissembling quiet in inquietness—

                                        III. xiii.

and so on. Revenge, awaked from sleep by Andrea's
ghost (an item which has been mistakenly ridiculed),
replies :

Sufficeth thee that poor Hieronimo
Cannot forget his son Horatio,
Nor dies Revenge although he sleep awhile.

                                        III. xii.

Bellimperia bitterly reproaches Hieronimo for his delay,
but he reassures her and plots on ; Isabella, committing

suicide, denounces his negligence ; but he is all the while at work. For Kyd, Hamlet was substantially in the same case ; and in making the prince excuse himself to the Ghost he is not implying that Hamlet has been really remiss. That is Shakespeare's development of the situation. Professor Bradley subtly argues [1] that when the Ghost says " Remember me " he is touching, not accidentally, on a faculty of forgetting known to him in Hamlet ; but in all probability the touch came from Kyd. When Jeronymo says (III. vi. 103) :

This makes me to *remember thee*, my son,

he does not mean that he had ever forgotten him.

§ 2. The Infusion of Pessimism.

The vital dramatic difference, however, between Jeronymo and Hamlet was that while the audience saw and followed Jeronymo's purpose, there was no very clear purpose in Kyd's Hamlet to follow. The question, put to this day by the unsophisticated, " Why doesn't he kill his uncle and live happy ever afterwards with Ophelia ? " was forestalled by Kyd only in so far as he offered the explanation given in the BRUDERMORD, that the King is always surrounded by his guards. That explanation, given him in the old story, probably seemed to him sufficient. But he in effect partly qualified it when, multiplying his episodes after his manner, he staged the play-scene, which put the King on his guard, and then the prayer-scene. If meantime, as we have surmised, there had been going on an action in connection

[1] *Shakespearean Tragedy*, p. 126.

with Fortinbras, Elizabethan audiences would be apt to be impatient.

True, once more, there has been no great delay in all: indeed, save for the indefinite interval between Acts I and II there has been none at all! The play-scene is only a day after the arrival of the players; and on that night the action rushes on to the point of the decreeing of Hamlet's voyage to England. After being convinced by the King's behaviour, Hamlet has had but one chance to slay him; and to stress that one recoil as the critics do is to pay a remarkable tribute to the " time-devouring " power of Shakespeare's dramatization. Hamlet, when all is said, is commonly condemned on the strength of a single recoil from assassination, and that under circumstances in which, religion apart, any high-minded man would have recoiled. To stab the King in the back while he knelt praying would have been truly a precious proof of " resolution " and " faculty for action." But the fact remains that, as Shakespeare's added soliloquies imply, the audiences, disregarding, under the dramatic spell, all questions of real time, fidgeted, without the modern critics to help them. They would have scouted the suggestion that a ghost was not a good witness; after the convincing play-scene they would grow suspicious; and after the prayer-scene many must have been moved to sarcasm, though doubtless Kyd's edifying theology impressed some. The broad fact is that, time apart, Hamlet as it were wilfully delays in our play, while Jeronymo is constantly planning his comprehensive vengeance, and loses no clear opportunity, though he too is slow, to the extent of angering his wife and Bellimperia.

Now, Shakespeare's handling of the play is above all

things a masterly effort to hint a psychological solution of the acted mystery, while actually heightening it by the self-accusing soliloquies. It is he who makes Hamlet keep the Ghost's tale secret: in the BRUDERMORD it is at once revealed to Horatio; and in our play we learn at the play-scene that it *had* been revealed in the interim. It is he who stresses the Queen's guilt, here reverting to the original story as against the treatment indicated in the BRUDERMORD, where the King makes no charge against his wife, though Hamlet speaks doubtfully of her at the close. In the First Quarto we have the Ghost's speech on the battlements from the text given in the Second; but in the closet-scene the Queen protests her absolute ignorance of the murder, and pledges herself, in lines that are obviously Kyd's, to assist Hamlet against the King. Here Kyd follows the Belleforest story, in which Geruth protests her innocence of the murder, saying nothing of other matters. In the Second Quarto these passages disappear, and though Hamlet does not accuse the Queen of complicity in the murder, his tone is that of one who has suffered tortures on the score of his mother's degradation.

This, if there be any, is the new ground note of Shakespeare's Hamlet. The guilt of a mother is an almost intolerable motive for drama, but it had to be maintained and emphasized to supply a psychological solution, or rather a hint of one. The childlike subserviency of poor Ophelia tells to the same effect.[1] Utter sickness of heart, revealing itself in pessimism, is again and again dramatically obtruded as if to set us feeling that for a heart so crushed revenge *is no remedy*.[2] And this implicit

[1] Professor Bradley's gallant and brilliant defence of the ill-starred child does not alter her relation to the action.
[2] Never that it is forbidden by religion.

pessimism is Shakespeare's personal contribution : his verdict on the situation set out by the play.[1] But the fact remains that he has not merely not been explicit— as he could not be—he has left standing matter which conflicts with the solution of pessimism ; he has exhibited Hamlet as roused to determination by the spectacle of the march of Fortinbras and declaring that he knows not why he has refrained ; and he has further exhibited him acting with abundant vigour in the sea episode, as he had previously done in planning the Court play. These displays of vigour, like the killing of Polonius, do not consist with a pessimism so laming as to preclude revenge. And the ultimate fact is that Shakespeare *could not* make a psychologically or otherwise consistent play out of a plot which retained a strictly barbaric action while the hero was transformed into a supersubtle Elizabethan.

§ 3. The Upshot.

If this be pronounced aspersive criticism, I have but to say that for me the play becomes only more wonderful

[1] Over thirty years ago I put the thesis of Hamlet's pessimism in an essay on *The Upshot of Hamlet* (1885). It has since been independently put by several German writers, who however leave the issue at that. See Hermann Türck's *Hamlet ein Genie*, 1888, and *Das psychologische Problem in der Hamlet-Tragödie*, 1890 ; also his polemic with Kuno Fischer over their respective originalities : *Die Uebereinstimmung von Kuno Fischer's und Hermann Türck's Hamlet-Erklärung*, 1894 ; and *Kuno Fischer's kritische Methode*, 1894. Both writers, as it happened, were repeating a British thesis. But Türck has the phrase : " Hamlet is the tragedy of idealism " (*Hamlet ein Genie*, p. 17), partly endorsed by Professor Bradley, p. 113. On the other hand, my proposition that Shakespeare imports a temporary pessimism of his own into Hamlet's situation was partly anticipated by Rümelin in his *Shakespearestudien*, 1866, p. 96 : " So war auch in Shakespeare die Hamlet-natur nur ein Theil seines Gemüthslebens." But he again was anticipated a century earlier by a British critic who far outwent his age in psychological penetration : " For what is Falstaff, what Lear, what Hamlet or Othello, but different modifications of Shakespeare's thought ? "—Maurice Morgann, *Essay on Falstaff*, 1777, p. 16.

when the manner of its evolution is realized. What Shakespeare could not do, no man could have done. What he did remains a miracle of dramatic imagination. In the place of one of the early and crude creations of Kyd, vigorous without verisimilitude,[1] outside of refined sympathy, he has projected a personality which from the first line sets all our sympathies in a quick vibration, and so holds our minds and hearts that even the hero's cruelties cannot alienate them. The triumph is achieved by sheer intensity of presentment, absolute lifelikeness of utterance, a thrilling and convincing rightness of phrase, and of feeling where wrong feeling is not part of the irremovable material. He who will may argue that Shakespeare should not have accepted intractable material. Let him tell us whether he would rather have been without HAMLET, and whether he cannot see that the practical compulsion to handle or retain intractable material underlies half a dozen of the Shakespeare plays as well as HAMLET,—TIMON, PERICLES, CYMBELINE, HENRY V, the WINTER'S TALE, MEASURE FOR MEASURE, ALL'S WELL, to say nothing of other comedies. Till that is seen, Shakespeare is not revealed.

He was, as usual, adapting an old play for his company, in the way of business. Its main features he had to preserve, else the public would miss what they looked for. HAMLET must retain its Ghost and its mock-madness, no less than the real madness of Ophelia. To satisfy the poet as well as his cultured patrons, the Prince must be made truly princely; and every stroke to that end was an element of success. But the revenge of the refined

---

[1] This, of course, does not apply to *Arden*, which is later, and psychologically very much superior to the *Tragedy*, though little better in point of verse technique.

Hamlet must be delayed as was that of the barbaric
Hamblet, without the original reason; the old machinery
must be retained, down to the prayer-scene; and so
there emerged a puzzling and unexplained character in
place of one analogous to the rudely and clearly outlined
Jeronymo, never puzzling to anybody save the characters
alongside him, who are not in his counsels as the
audience are.

Evolving a Hamlet of the highest mental lucidity,
Shakespeare himself at one point accepted the inference
of an " almost blunted purpose," a will that will not act
when it should; and by a score of subtle strokes he
tacitly suggests how a man may feel the barrenness of
a revenge to which he is vowed. But this is only half
of his composite Hamlet: the other is the presentment
of a man who can act with lightning speed and force,
and will " make a ghost of him that lets me." Of all
the explanatory formulas, that of Mackenzie, so little
discussed, is the best.[1] He posits an excess of sensibility
which yields uncertain and divergent action—a spirit
which recoils as uncontrollably from straightforward
killing as from another's villany or unworthiness. With
a difference, Professor Bradley pronounces that Hamlet
" tries to find reasons for his delay in pursuing a design
which excites his aversion."[2] Such a conception may
as easily be read into Shakespeare as that of psychic
shock, or pessimism arising out of personal disillusion-
ment. But it also is inadequate to the data. Hamlet
thrusts through the arras without hesitation, and shows
no horror at his deed. He has no scruple about sending

[1] The essay on *Hamlet* is not included in the collected edition of
Mackenzie's *Miscellaneous Works*, 3 vols. 1820.
[2] *Shakespearean Tragedy*, p. 226.

his schoolfellows to their death on the bare surmise that
they knew the contents of the King's dispatch. A " sensibility " which yields at once these results and an insuperable recoil from vengeance on a villain is not finally
thinkable. In the words of Salvini, " A man like Hamlet
has never existed, nor could exist."[1] This, as we must
admit in the conclusion, is not really an ultimate indictment of Shakespeare : but it is a necessary estoppel of
certain theorists who turn an æsthetic suggestion into
a false historic theorem.

When, on the other hand, we can see so clearly how
Shakespeare was artistically committed to a series of
barbaric actions which had nothing to do with either
sensibility or pessimism, but which he had yet to assign
to a prince in whom sensibility and pessimism were
artistically developed by himself for the very purpose
of dramatic verisimilitude, it is idle to follow the dogged
defensive tactics of Werder, who was determined to find
a consistent whole where such does not exist.

The whole of Werder's polemic, as we saw, is a defiance
of the two vital soliloquies (II. end ; IV. iv.) in which
Hamlet impeaches himself. To call these, as Werder
does, " protests against the circumstances," is to do
sheer violence to the text. Hebler was able to confute
the thesis on the sole basis of the first,[2] convicting Werder
of grotesque misconstructions—partly due, it may be,
to the translation he followed.[3] But Hebler's own
solution was only less unsatisfying. Insisting on the
subjective solution, he formulated a " defective com-

[1] Art. " Salvini on Shakespeare," by Helen Zimmern, *Gentleman's
Magazine*, February 1884.
[2] Art. *Die Hamletfrage*, in *Im neuen Reich*, 1875, No. 41.
[3] Cp. *The Heart of Hamlet's Mystery*, note by translator, p. 44.

mingling of blood and judgment," [1] resulting not in a defect of will but in a defect of efficiency—" not a Will-not but a Can-not," " grounded in his [Hamlet's] personality." [2] This formula in turn merely evades the many instances in which Hamlet *can* act with instant and decisive force ; and we are left with nothing better than the nugatory notion that a man cannot do what he does not do. The problem of the play is merely baulked : we get an argument in a circle.

The German battle-royal of the seventh and eighth decades of last century is in fact but a protracted process of thesis-seeking, in which every device is tried to explain the problem without looking to its genesis. Rümelin, who came nearest doing so, was biassed by his purpose of combating " Shakespeare-Mania " and convicting the idol of clay feet, or at least clay toes. Rightly turning back to the old saga for the starting-point, he wrongly reasoned that all the difference between that and the final play is of Shakespeare's making ; never inquiring how fresh foundations may have been laid in the intermediate play, though he actually refers [3] to the First Quarto, and might by comparing that with the BRUDER-MORD, in the light of the Kyd-hypothesis, have seen the necessity of reckoning with other determinants than the saga and Shakespeare. Rightly enough he pronounces the play to have been often retouched ; and he makes the very intelligent suggestion that the duplication of Hamlet's fooling with Polonius and Osric cannot have been original, but must have come of a readjustment, what was intended as a substitution of effects being by oversight allowed to result in a repetition. But he sees

[1] Art. cited, p. 562. [2] *Id.* p. 571.
[3] *Shakespearestudien*, 1866, p. 90.

nothing of the pre-Shakespearean construction, and so gets by a leap to the theory of "an unsatisfactory inter-weaving of an episodical, modern-subjective element in the old-northern saga"[1] (a theory which, he avows, will not untie all the knots), laying the whole procedure at Shakespeare's door.

Hebler countered Rümelin by a *tu quoque!* He summed up that in Rümelin's view Shakespeare sought (1) primarily and ostensibly to represent the saga-Hamlet and not a loiterer (*Saümer*); (2) but, as suited him best, at the same time a creature of his own spiritual cast; and (3) was thus compelled to make him a loiterer, albeit one who reproached himself for being so. To which Hebler retorted that Rümelin himself had gone through the experience he ascribes to Shakespeare: that Rümelin began (1) with the saga-Hamlet, but found himself (2) caught by the idea of Shakespeare's introduction of his own personality into the matter; and so was led to the third view—of Hamlet as a self-reproaching loiterer—by way of modifying positions first and second.[2] However that may be, Rümelin ends in sheer arbitrariness when he pronounces that Shakespeare's Hamlet differs from the barbarian in that "he must end tragically, *like all the figures* in which the poet has poured perilous stuff (*Krankheitstoff*) out of his own mental life—like Werther, Clavigo, Faust, Eduard."[3] As we know, Shakespeare's Hamlet simply had to end tragically because the play was a tragedy to begin with.

All the while, Rümelin was at one point nearer the true line of criticism than Hebler, inasmuch as, in Hebler's words, he substituted a thesis of "Faults of

---

[1] *Id.* p. 87.   [2] *Aufsätze*, as cited, pp. 214–15.
[3] *Shakespearestudien*, p. 96.

the Poet " for that of " Faults of the Hero." It was much sounder than Werder's " Faults of the Situation " ; and only needed revision and development to yield a " positive " critical method. But among them the German combatants reached no solid ground ; and Rümelin, who became unfairly identified with the " Anti-Shakespeare-maniacs " who followed, is not even named by Max J. Wolff in his outline-list of German critical pronouncements on HAMLET.

That writer in turn, who ranks as the leading Shakespeare critic in latter-day Germany, carries the geocentric principle of interpretation to a height of fantastic complexity which it is to be hoped will be the signal for a resort, even in Germany, to positive methods.

Rejecting Goethe's formula as the most unfit of all, and ignoring Werder's, he combines a whole series of subjective solutions with a new one to the effect that Hamlet is the representative of *Truth* against a world of falsities, which at the same time he cancels by the added formula that Hamlet " *will not* " act. His exposition works out, in brief, thus :

1. " At one stroke the rôles of the tragedy are distributed " (in the " seems, madam," speech) : " Here Hamlet as representative of Truth ; on the other side the court, the world of show." Hamlet stands alone with Horatio and the despised players. " To them, the professional cultivators of show, Truth must take her flight, for all other *milieus* are closed to her." " After your death you were better have a bad epitaph than their ill report while you live " ;—*because* " *then* the comedians are the voice of Truth " (!).

2. Hamlet sets himself to be the reformer of the *time* —to put right the disjointed world.

3. "But this is not to be accomplished by man, or by Hamlet, but without him, or against him, only through the indwelling moral power of Truth."

3a. A God is needed to fulfil the mission.

4. A great tragic irony lies in the exposition.   All human foresight is fruitless.

5. The Prince reacts to every new impression. [Mackenzie's formula, unconsciously adopted.]

6. He is a dilettant.   [What else could a prince be ?]

7. Having had no discipline of duty, therefore, he is "himself an enigma," and therefore he refuses when for the first time duty enters his life with her behests.

1a. Yet the moral ideal within him makes him worthy to be the champion of Truth, however many human failings he may also have.

8. Pessimism, however, had already overwhelmed him.

9. So his uncle's crime does not appear to him as one man's guilt.   All mankind is responsible for it.

9a. "His pessimism shuts out for him the knowledge that in the person of the crowned murderer he can and should tear up the root of the evil.   He lets pass the moment indicated (*gewiesenen*) by Fate.   [Which ?] . . . he neglects doing what he should and can, to hang on to it plans for world-betterment which overpass human powers."   [Where does he so plan ?]

10. "Hamlet *will not* avenge his private wrong.   As to this he is quite clear from the start."   He shows it by the entry in his tables (!).[1]

8a. "This appeals to his mood, as consummating his

[1] This verdict is also given by Professor Trench.

pessimism, which under all outward show has scented corruption."

10a. "Because he *will not* act, because he *will not* undertake the plainly prescribed deed laid upon him, he will tell his friends nothing." [How then comes he to tell Horatio later?]

10b. "Hamlet relates himself quite passively to his task. He *cannot* reform the world; he *will not* punish his uncle." [1]

These, I think, are all the motives and explanations, put in their sequence. It seems impossible to put more "points in Hamlet's soul": the geocentric method has been diligently exhausted. And it is all to no purpose. Formulas which are in conflict cannot be reduced to unity by imposing either a general formula of Truth-seeking which would equally apply to LEAR and OTHELLO, and is therefore neutral to all, or an arbitrary "will not" formula which is never given save by reducing to the form of an accusation the perplexity set up by the delay in the action. The delay was there from the start, as the dramatic datum of an original action in which there was no thought of Truth *versus* Show, or World-Betterment, or overruling Providence, or over-susceptibility, or pessimism, or the fatality of dilettantism in princes, or the refusal of the hero to act. The motive of the original story is to follow the hero's *way* of acting. This remains the motive of Kyd, who, however, by altering the basis fatally confuses the movement. Shakespeare, by immensely heightening the character, puts it in still further irrelation to the action, giving us one great satisfaction in forgoing another.

[1] *Shakespeare, der Dichter und sein Werk*, von Max J. Wolff, 3te Aufl, 1913, ii. 120–7.

It is true that he *indicates* over-sensibility, and a pessimism which makes action seem vain; but he also presents other and contrary things, and he *could not* indicate a "will not" which would cancel all the rest of the play, or a "plan" of reforming the world which would explode it. He can be clearly seen inserting soliloquies which absolutely posit the *need* for an explanation. That at the end of the third Act is a self-impeachment by Hamlet which avows as much; and it is clearly an addition made without close heed to what goes before; for Hamlet talks of arranging for a play as if he had not already arranged one with the players—unless that previous arrangement is itself an addition which takes no note of the soliloquy.[1] So with the soliloquy at the passage of the army of Fortinbras, an expedient of the same kind, designed to satisfy or pacify the auditors who wanted to know why Hamlet did not commit the right murder instead of the wrong one. Of course it could not satisfy; and, inserted as it is in the Second Quarto, we find it dropped from the Folio, evidently as having been dropped from the prompter's copies. Written

---

[1] Professor Trench confidently argues (pp. 109, 111, 122, 124, 160, 225, *note*) that after arranging to supply the players with a new speech for *The Murder of Gonzago* Hamlet "resolves to substitute for that an original play of his own composition." This will not stand. The play finally *is* "The Murder of Gonzago" (III. ii. 249, 273, 275); and Hamlet instructs the player to "speak *the speech* . . . as I pronounced it to you." In the First Quarto the players are "the Duke and Dutchesse," not "King and Queen" as in the Second and in the Folio. To say that in the actual play-scene he "changes the name of his *Mousetrap* to that of a play that was before his mind on the previous day" is quite unwarrantable; the "name" is a jesting one spontaneously thrown out, not the real title of a new piece. Not that we are necessarily to suppose that there *was* such a play, though there may have been [Albertus is the Duke's name in Q. 1: and "Lucianus, nephew to the King," seems to mean "to the King of Guyana," which there takes the place of "Vienna"]; but that the thesis of Hamlet's inability to keep to any plan is gratuitous. The *dramatist* is the factor.

in Shakespeare's vividest verse, it does but aggravate the perplexity by assuming that Hamlet has much need to excuse himself, and avowing that he cannot. Instead of suggesting or sanctioning a theory of either subjective or objective hindrance, it negates both. It is almost as if the dramatist, anticipating Lowell and Professor Trench and the rest, were censuring his own adopted creature. But that, of course, is not Shakespeare's way. He has simply decided to accept inexplicable delay as the formula of a play which reached him with that character apparently stamped upon it.

For it is idle to pretend that Shakespeare was deeply concerned to secure perfect artistic consistency. As an adaptor and reconstructor he worked wonders; but he had to let pass many incongruities, in many plays. To those already noted we may add the retention of the Dumb Show, in which, before the play, the murder is enacted even as it is after the speeches. As it is the action and not the speaking that upsets the King, he ought either to have been upset by the Dumb Show or to have collected himself for the repetition.[1] Shakespeare at this point merely let stand what he found, as he let stand the episodes which we have seen to be " out of the frame." Whether or not by reason of the play being originally in two parts, it is full of fortuitous retardations; and it is not surprising that in a recent revival the actor-manager dropped such matters as the advice to the players and Polonius' advice to Laertes; even as the Reynaldo scene had been dropped long before.

It is possible, indeed, to exaggerate the incongruities of the piece. Though Hamlet's age is certainly a conundrum, Professor Bradley has perhaps made needless

[1] This was commented on a century ago

difficulty [1] as to Hamlet's proposed return to Wittenberg. " Going *back* to school in Wittenberg " does not necessarily mean that he has just come thence ; and his reception of Horatio and Marcellus does not imply, as Professor Bradley says, that he and Horatio are supposed to have left Wittenberg " for Elsinore less than two months ago." Hamlet may have left it years before ; and his " Horatio, or I do forget myself," suggests long severance. As Professor Trench remarks, " the city " may very well be Copenhagen, where Hamlet may have spent time after leaving Wittenberg. But there is real incongruity in his telling Horatio (III. ii.) how he has prized him " since my dear soul was mistress of her choice," after greeting him with " Horatio—or I do forget myself." Even Professor Trench, who assures us that Shakespeare is " regular and orderly in his work with the regularity and order of a classical genius," [2] and warns us that when we fail to understand it may be our own fault,[3] also declares [4] that " when we fail to understand him [Shakespeare], it certainly is often his own fault."

It is most true, if we must say " fault " in a case, where the master is performing a miracle of transmutation, vitalizing, elevating and irradiating a crude creation into a world's wonder, and finally missing artistic consistency simply because consistency was absolutely excluded by the material. He leaves it possible for some (including Professor Trench) to think Hamlet more or less really mad. He indicates no totally explanatory formula because he could not : the play will not now go into any. In paying ourselves with saving formulas of Hamlet's mystery we are but obscuring Shakespeare's mystery, which

---

[1] In Note B on *Hamlet* in *Shakespearean Tragedy.*
[2] P. 187.   [3] P. 166.   [4] P. 109.

is here finally so legible and so vividly interesting. HAMLET
is only the more wonderful for being rightly " understood."
When Furnivall indignantly rejected [1] the thesis of the
Clarendon Press editors that the First Quarto in its
construction is mainly the work of the earlier playwright,
he was but revealing the uncritical temper of the older
Shakespeare-worship. Disregarding the real tests of
diction and psychology, he was staking Shakespeare's
greatness on such positions as the invention of the idea
of a play-within-the-play and the creation of such dialogue as Hamlet's " chaff " with Polonius—work within
the capacity of lesser men than Kyd. The assailed editors
had made a loyal induction from the documents ; and
Furnivall and Dowden, refusing to make it, were seeking
for Shakespeare the wrong kind of credit. His real
triumph was to turn a crude play into the masterpiece
which he has left us. It is a perfectly magnificent *tour
de force*, and its ultimate æsthetic miscarriage is only
the supreme illustration of the vulgar but ancient truth
that an entirely satisfactory silken purse cannot be
constructed, even by a Shakespeare, out of a sow's ear
—if one can without indecency apply that figure to a
barbaric saga which ultimately yielded us HAMLET.

Æsthetically, it is improper. For, when all is said,
the " pragmatic " test is practically final for such a thing
as a drama. HAMLET has " made good " : it has enor-
mously overpassed the simple end of the playwright, to
entertain. The miraculous puppetry of the actor-manager
has kept millions at gaze for centuries now ; and if
Shakespeare could be recreated and asked why he managed
here and there so oddly, he might with an unanswerable
effect open eyes of wonder and ask what should make

[1] *Academy,* August 7, 1880.

us thus put his mechanism to the rack. " Do you want an *absolute*," he might ask, " as a stage entertainment ? " And though we might make play with Hamlet's dictum about holding up a mirror to Nature, we should be met by the reminder that that too is part of the *play* ; and we should know that Shakespeare had non-suited us.

And so he might silence us if we sought to debate with him on the character of Iago, which in Professor Bradley's fine dissection we almost feel to be drawn from life itself. " Did you mean to make a study of moral insanity ? " we might ask him : " is the formula of Iago simply that he is at bottom *the* criminal type, crafty in will-worship and stupid in craft—a reversion to the ape or savage ? " " Does that really matter ? " he might reply. " Has not the play sufficed to *occupy* intelligent people ? What matters it whether Iago could or could not have really existed ? Could Othello ? Could Falstaff ? For that matter, could *any* imagined person ? What *is* fiction ? . . . The play works. Would anything but Iago serve to drive a tragedy that hinges on a handkerchief ? If you think so, try another." And there an end.

But the critical intellect too has its rights : *its* concern is simply conceptual truth ; and as against—*not* Shakespeare but—those who formulate Ptolemaic schemes of his works, its rights are absolute. The " purpose of playing is "—well, not exactly what Hamlet-Shakespeare alleges ! But the purpose of science is indisputably to know how things actually went ; and it is time we had done with Ptolemaic methods, though the literary Ptolemaists have included some remarkably able men, recalling the distinguished prototype, who was a very able man indeed.

INDEX

A SELECTION OF BOOKS

ISSUED BY

GEORGE ALLEN & UNWIN LTD.

Out and About

London in War-time   BY THOMAS BURKE

Crown 8vo.   5*s.* net.   *Postage 6d.*

"A delightful . . . joyous . . . lusty little volume. We have many writers of essays in England now, but none has quite the sparkling zest in crowded life which is so marked a quality of Mr. Burke. His enjoyment of 'London with the many sins' is in lineal descent from Lamb's, and it is far wider."—*Times.*

"A delightful book which Dickens might have written. Thomas Burke is a realist, with a quick sense of the pathos and humour of life, and a subtle charm of style . . . his comment on people and places is as shrewd and piquant as are his swift, graphic descriptions of them."—*Sketch.*

"Mr. Bnrke is our greatest living authority on the urban vagabond and the master of a style as beguiling as Murger's. . . . Mr. Burke's delightful book. . . which the gentle Elia would have loved as a bed-book."—*Morning Post.*

"An extraordinarily vivid little volume. Scarcely a paragraph which does not hold some extraordinary bit of description, a word picture painted by a writer of genius. . . as it were Brangwyn drawings done into prose."—*Tatler.*

"Mr. Burke's literary reputation is one of the very few that have been made since 1914. Humour is in his basket as well as horror. Evidently a young man to watch."—*Daily Mail.*

An Ethiopian Saga

BY RICHMOND HAIGH

Foolscap 8vo.   5*s.* net.

"Extremely interesting . . . a book quite out of the common, both in form and substance."—*Times.*

"A great success. Sir Rider Haggard has never done anything equal in this way to Mr. Haigh's terrific and yet most pathetic fight between Mataaw and Bokalobi."—*Evening News.*

"Has the charm of complete novelty. . . unusual freshness and a curious fascination of style. Its simple thought and often the great natural beauty of its imagery and its depth of feeling ought to bring the book many readers who will appreciate its charm."—*Liverpool Post.*

The Helping Hand

An Essay in Philosophy and Religion for the Unhappy

Crown 8vo. Stiff Covers. By GERALD GOULD   3s. net.

"A philosopher with a deeply religious conscience. . . . There must be many people to whom this little book will bring comfort."—J. D. BERESFORD, in the *Saturday Westminster.*

"A book that helps. . . . I welcome it with great joy."—MAUDE ROYDEN, in *The Herald.*

"Will appeal to many whom the professional theologian and preacher cannot touch."—*The Christian Commonwealth.*

Poems Written During the Great War, 1914—1918

AN ANTHOLOGY EDITED BY BERTRAM LLOYD

Cr. 8vo. Paper Boards.   SECOND IMPRESSION   2s. 6d. net.

"Written by members of all the belligerent nations, they testify that certain sentiments are common to the just and the unjust."—*Outlook.*

"We have had a good many anthologies of war poetry, and Bertram Lloyd's is quite one of the best."—*Sketch.*

The Best of Both Worlds

Poems of Spirit and Sense

By HENRY VAUGHAN AND ANDREW MARVELL
(1621–1695)   (1621–1678)

EDITED BY FRANCIS MEYNELL

In Decorative Paper Boards. 7½" × 4¼". 2ND IMPRESSION. 3s. net.

"One of the most charming anthologies imaginable."—*Daily News.*

Young Heaven   By MILES MALLESON

Crown 8vo. Paper Covers.   3s. 6d. net.

"An eloquent exposition of the relations of art and morality."—*Manchester Guardian.*

Monogamy   By GERALD GOULD

Crown 8vo. Stiff Covers.   SECOND IMPRESSION   2s. net.

"One of the most remarkable books published this year."—*Everyman.*

"Full of passionate thought and living imagination."—*Common Cause.*

"Abounds in felicitous phrasing and quaintly satiric lines."—*New Witness.*

WORKS BY
GILBERT MURRAY, LL.D., D.LITT.

Regius Professor of Greek in the University of Oxford

THE PLAYS OF EURIPIDES. Translated into English Rhyming Verse, with Commentaries and Explanatory Notes. Cloth, 2/6 net each. Paper, 1/6 net each ; or the first six plays in two vols. 6/- net each.

HIPPOLYTUS. *20th Thousand*	MEDEA.	*8th Thousand*
BACCHAE. *16th Thousand*	IPHIGENIA IN TAURIS.	
THE TROJAN WOMEN.		*13th Thousand*
15th Thousand	RHESUS.	*3rd Thousand*
THE ELECTRA. *13th Thousand*	ALCESTIS.	*6th Thousand*

OEDIPUS, KING OF THEBES. By SOPHOCLES. *14th Thousand*

THE FROGS OF ARISTOPHANES. *12th Thousand*

EURIPIDES : *Hippolytus ; Bacchae ; Aristophanes' "Frogs."* With an Appendix on *The Lost Tragedies of Euripides*, an Introduction on *The Significance of the Bacchae in Athenian History*, and 12 Illustrations from Ancient Sculptures. *Seventh Edition.* Crown 8vo. Cloth, gilt top, 7/6 net.

ANDROMACHE : An Original Play in Three Acts. Cloth, 2/6 net ; Paper, 1/6 net. *Third Impression.*

THE WAY FORWARD : Three Articles on Liberal Policy. Introduction by VISCOUNT GREY OF FALLODON, K.G. Demy 8vo. Paper Covers, 1/- net.

THE STOIC PHILOSOPHY. Fcap. 8vo. Cloth, 1/3 net. Paper, 9d. net.

RELIGIO GRAMMATICI : The Religion of a Man of Letters. Fcap. 8vo. Paper, 1/- net. Cloth, 1/6 net. *Third Impression.*

ARISTOPHANES AND THE WAR PARTY. Fcap. 8vo. Paper, 1/- net. Cloth, 1/6 net.

THE GREEK TRADITION. Essays in the Reconstruction of Ancient Thought. By J. A. K. THOMSON. Preface by GILBERT MURRAY. Crown 8vo. 6/- net.

Printed in Great Britain by
UNWIN BROTHERS, LIMITED
WOKING AND LONDON

Lightning Source UK Ltd.
Milton Keynes UK
UKOW011853251112

202751UK00004B/38/P